Berlitz®
Ireland

Text by Ken B.
Updated and edi...
Picture...
M...

Berlitz POCKET GUIDE

Ireland

Seventh Edition 2004

NO part of this book may be reproduced, stored in a retrieval system or transmitted in any form or means electronic, mechanical, photocopying, recording or otherwise, without prior written permission from Berlitz Publishing. Brief text quotations with use of photographs are exempted for book review purposes only.

PHOTOGRAPHY

Collections/Image Ireland/Bob Brien 78; Jason Mitchell 53; Richard Nowitz 3CL, 10, 11, 24, 27, 29, 31, 34, 38, 91, 101; Doug Plummer 16, 32, 40, 43, 51, 54, 58, 63, 64, 66, 68, 76, 88, 90, 92, 96, 99; Geray Sweeney 2B, 3CT, 3C, 6, 14, 19, 22, 25, 36, 41, 50, 61, 70, 75, 79, 80, 81, 82, 85, 98, 100, 102; Tophani Picturepoint 20; Marcus Wilson-Smith 1, 8, 35, 45, 47, 48, 49, 52, 56, 71, 72, 84, 86, 94; Courtesy of The Green Gate, Donegal 77
Cover picture: Doug Plummer

CONTACTING THE EDITORS

Every effort has been made to provide accurate information in this publication, but changes are inevitable. The publisher cannot be responsible for any resulting loss, inconvenience or injury. We would appreciate it if readers would call our attention to any errors or outdated information by contacting Berlitz Publishing, PO Box 7910, London SE1 1WE, England. Fax: (44) 20 7403 0290;
e-mail: berlitz@apaguide.co.uk
www.berlitzpublishing.com

All Rights Reserved

© 2004 Apa Publications GmbH & Co. Verlag KG, Singapore Branch, Singapore

Printed in Singapore by Insight Print Services (Pte) Ltd, 38 Joo Koon Road, Singapore 628990.
Tel: (65) 6865-1600. Fax: (65) 6861-6438

Berlitz Trademark Reg. U.S. Patent Office and other countries. Marca Registrada

Galway's city centre (page 67) is the place to head for traditional pubs, seafood and salty air

A product of Ireland's monastic heritage, the Book of Kells at Trinity College, Dublin (page 26) is wonderfully ornate

The ancient monastery at Glendalough (page 41) lies in a spectacular setting

TOP TEN ATTRACTIONS

Temple Bar
(page 30),
the lively hub
of Dublin's
nightlife

The idyllic Dingle Peninsula
(page 61) lives up to visitors'
romantic notions of Ireland

The Crown Liquor Saloon
(page 81) in Belfast has a
magnificent tiled interior and
beautifully carved private snugs

The countryside and coastline of
Donegal (page 76) have a wild beauty
that hasn't been spoiled by tourism

Cork (page 52), the
Republic's second city, has
an old-fashioned charm

You can find a
continental air
along Dublin's
Grafton Street
(page 26)

Newgrange's burial
chambers (page
37) form a major
prehistoric site

CONTENTS

A ➤ in the text denotes a highly recommended sight

INTRODUCTION

The grass really does grow greener in Ireland – it's not called the 'Emerald Isle' for nothing, although the rain-drenched verdant pastures alternate with plains of grain, bleak and rugged hills, mountains and soggy bogs. The quick-changing sky adds to the drama of the encounter between land and sea. You will never be further than 115km (70 miles) from Ireland's dramatic 4,800-km (3,000-mile) coastline. Far to the west lies America, a beacon for countless emigrants during the 19th century. To the east lies Britain, whose relationship with its next-door neighbour has for 800 years been one of the most infuriatingly complex in European geopolitics.

The proximity of the Gulf Stream keeps winters mild. Snow is rare, rain is not. Significant rainfall is recorded on three out of every four days near the west coast, and on every second day in the east, and ranges from stormy

> More than 5 million people live on the island – fewer than before the great potato famine of the 1840s. Emigration was high until recently, but now the population is finally on the rise.

torrents to refreshing mist so nebulous that it leaves the pavement unmarked. The sun is never far behind the rain, however, and the slightest shower has always been a fine excuse for an Irish rainbow.

There are, of course, two Irelands: the 26 counties of the Republic of Ireland (Éire) and the six counties of the British-governed Northern Ireland. This gives the island two capitals: Dublin and Belfast. In Dublin, a lively city of broad avenues, green parks and harmonious, ordered terraces,

Showing off Gaelic football loyalties on a lamppost in Belfast

The green, green grass of Kinsale

there is more in the way of museums, galleries and other cultural attractions than in many cities of comparable size, plus a delightfully subversive sense of humour that some would say conceals a deep sense of fatalism. In contrast, Belfast is Ireland's only industrial centre and its energy is more grounded and less subtle than Dublin's.

By and large, though, the truly inspiring sights of Ireland are found outside the big towns. Ireland is still rooted in agriculture and, as you travel by car or bus from one town to the next, you will pass through miles of farmland generously populated with sheep and cattle. Natural wonders in Ireland can be as awesome as the Cliffs of Moher, or as tranquil as the Lakes of Killarney; as mystical as the holy mountain of Croagh Patrick, or as delightful as the horse-breeding prairie of the Curragh. Scattered amidst these natural beauties stand impressive stone relics which date back thousands of years. In Ireland, the concept of a town is not much more than a thousand years old. Before then, the island was almost entirely rural, and its now-ancient buildings often began as monastic settlements that kept learning alive in Europe during the Dark Ages.

This is a small country but, like vintage wine, it should be savoured slowly. A signpost may present you with three ways of getting to a destination, or it may show none. Ask a passer-by, and, if they decide you look a bit weary after a hard day's sightseeing and comparing pints of Guinness, they'll probably reassure you that it's 'just a wee way ahead' because they won't wish to distress you by telling you it's really 32km (20 miles) by a narrow, twisting road.

The Irish

There is no single 'Irish' character. The Northern Protestant is generally regarded as being more earnest and less imaginative than the Northern Catholic, who in turn is seen as more introverted and less impulsive than the Southern Catholic. The Irish refine these distinctions even further, giving the sense of place an importance seldom found elsewhere in the world.

More than 1½ million people live in Dublin, the largest city in the Republic of Ireland and home to more than 40 percent of its population. Belfast, with a population of 500,000, is the hub of Northern Ireland, which remained a part of the United Kingdom when the island was partitioned after World War I. The new republic, whose birth pangs in 1922 included a civil war, settled down to being a predominantly rural economy, with social affairs and its education system strongly influenced by the Roman Catholic church.

Where There's Smoke

The characteristic smell of peat fires pervades much of Ireland's countryside. Since the 17th century the bogs have been exploited as an inexpensive source of fuel. During the great potato famine (1845–51) dried peat was often the only fuel available. In recent times, more efficient methods of cutting the peat have put an extra strain on Irish bogs and, although peat fires smell lovely in winter, the remaining bogs are to be protected from further digging.

In the final quarter of the 20th century, as Northern Ireland was suffering political turmoil, the South set about transforming itself into a modern European state. Membership of the European Union provided great economic benefits, and tax incentives were strategically used to attract European and American industries, primarily in the high-tech and pharmaceutical sectors. The old taboos on divorce and abortion began to fade away as the influence of the church declined. A strong youth culture turned Dublin into a party town targeted for weekend breaks by Europe's budget airlines,

A Native Tongue

The historic Anglo-Norman conquest of Ireland in 1169 paved the way for the supremacy of the English language over Gaelic. Nowadays, scarcely one in a hundred people in Ireland speaks Irish more fluently than English. However,

Celebrating Bloomsday, an annual homage to James Joyce's *Ulysses*

reviving Gaelic has become state policy; it is taught in schools and printed (along with English) on all official signs and documents. Everyday use of Gaelic is limited to the Gaeltacht areas – small pockets of native culture which are predominantly in the west of the island. Gaelic's vocabulary, intonation and sentence structures have infiltrated English, creating great literature and lending everyday speech patterns a touch of poetry.

Stained-glass window in Belfast's City Hall

The Northern Counties

For the last three decades of the 20th century, the image of Northern Ireland was blighted by terrorists, who aspired to unite its six counties with the Republic's 26. Today, although tribal animosities can still be ignited, a somewhat tetchy harmony prevails much of the time and the substantial subsidies poured into the region from Britain, the European Union and the United States have created a relative prosperity, though unemployment remains high.

Two things have been insufficiently appreciated: the down-to-earth friendliness of the people (towards outsiders, anyway) and the spectacular scenery – any other country combining the allure of the Antrim Coast Road, the Giant's Causeway, the lakes of Fermanagh, the Mountain of Mourne and a wealth of golf courses would sink under the weight of tourists. But, in the end, confounding expectations is something at which both parts of the island effortlessly excel.

A BRIEF HISTORY

Stone-Age relics reveal that Ireland has been inhabited for at least 8,000 years. The first settlers probably travelled on foot from Scandinavia to Scotland – England was linked at that time to northern Europe by land – then across what was a narrow sea gap to Ireland.

During the late Stone Age, inhabitants began to settle down and farm. Tombs and temples from this period can be found across the country. These monuments may be simple stone tripods in the middle of a farmer's field, or they can be sophisticated passage-graves built on astronomical principles and decorated with mysterious spiral and zigzag engravings.

Portrait of Christ from the 9th-century Book of Kells

New settlers introduced Bronze-Age skills from Europe, but by the time of the Iron Age Ireland was lagging behind the Continent. This technology did not reach the island until the last years of the pre-Christian era, thanks to Celtic tribes from central Europe.

The Roman legions that rolled across Western Europe into Britain stopped short at the Irish Sea. The island was left free to develop its own way of life during the centuries of the great Roman Empire. Though Irish society was decentralised into scores of bickering mini-kingdoms, a single culture did develop. Druids and poets told legends in a common language that is clearly recognisable as the Irish version of Gaelic.

St Patrick's Day

The Celts frequently staged raids on Roman Britain for booty and slaves. During one 5th-century raid, they rounded up a large number of captives to ease the manpower shortage. One of these 'immigrants', a 16-year-old boy named Patrick, later became Ireland's national saint. After spending a few years as a humble shepherd, he escaped to Gaul, became a monk, and finally returned to convert 'the heathens' to Christianity.

St Patrick developed a system of monasteries to serve as the centre for all church activities. This suited life in Ireland – a rural and skimpily populated island with diverse power centres.

St Patrick's crusade was a unique triumph. Ireland was the only Western European country where the people were converted without a single Christian being martyred.

While the rest of Europe crawled through the Dark Ages, the Irish monasteries kept the flame of Western culture alight. Scholarly minds from different regions of Europe converged on the island to participate in its religious and intellectual life. The monks of the 'island of saints and scholars' dutifully created illuminated manuscripts copied from abroad. These books are now some of Ireland's most valuable works of art.

The Vikings

At the turn of the 9th century, well-armed warriors sailed in from Scandinavia aboard sleek boats. The undefended Irish monasteries, full of relics and treasures, were easy targets.

The shallow-draught ships moved in and attacked virtually at will, making their way around the Irish coast and up its rivers as well. This danger inspired multi-storey 'round towers', which variously served as watch-towers, belfries, store-houses, and escape hatches. Dozens still stand. But plunder wasn't the only thing on the Viking agenda: they soon added trading colonies around the coast and founded the first towns on the rural island – Dublin, Waterford and Limerick.

The Irish learned sailing, weaponry and metalworking from the Norse, but resented their presence. In the end, the natives ousted the Vikings, with the last struggle taking

Ireland's Viking heritage is remembered in Dublin

place in 1014 at the Battle of Clontarf, when the High King of Ireland, Brian Ború, defeated the tough Norse and their Irish allies. although he himself was killed in the battle.

Rivalry and Revenge

Ireland's next invasion was motivated by jealousy. In 1152, the wife of Tiernan O'Rourke, an Irish warrior-king, was carried off by rival Dermot MacMurrough of Leinster. Allegedly the lady was a willing victim, possibly even the instigator. Regardless, O'Rourke got his queen back a few months later, but wasn't about to forgive and forget. He forced Dermot to flee, in 1166, first to England and then France. But from there, Dermot was able to shape an alliance with a powerful Norman nobleman, the Earl of Pembroke. The Earl, known as Strongbow, agreed to lead an army to sweep Dermot back to power. In exchange, the Earl was to be given the hand of Dermot's daughter and the right to succeed him to the Leinster throne. The hardy Normans – the elite of Europe's warriors – won the Battle of Waterford in 1169, and Strongbow married his princess in Waterford's grand cathedral.

In further engagements, the Norman war machine stunned and swiftly defeated Norse and Irish forces. Things were going so well for Strongbow that his overlord, King Henry II of England, arrived in 1171 to assert his sovereignty.

The English Ascendancy

The Anglo-Norman occupation brought profound and long-lasting changes. Towns, churches and castles were built alongside institutions for feudal government. There was much resentment among the Irish, but for the colonial rulers the challenge of revolt was less serious than the danger of total cultural assimilation. With settlers adopting the ways of the natives, rather than the other way round, the Statutes of Kilkenny were introduced in 1366, banning inter-marriage and forbidding the English from speaking Gaelic.

English control was consolidated when the House of Tudor turned its attention to Ireland. Henry VIII, the first English monarch to be titled 'King of Ireland', introduced the Reformation to Ireland as well as England, but the new religion of Protestantism took root only in the Pale (the area around Dublin) and in the large provincial towns under English control. In the rest of Ireland, Catholic monasteries carried on as before, as did the Irish language.

From the mid-16th century, the implementation of the so-called plantation policy heralded the large-scale redistribu-

The huge influence of the Catholic church has declined only recently

tion of wealth. Desirable farmland was confiscated from Catholics and given to Protestant settlers. During the Reign of Elizabeth I revolts were widespread, but the most unyielding resistance was in the northeastern province of Ulster, where chiefs formed an alliance with Spain – the Queen's bitterest enemy. In 1601, a Spanish mini-armada sailed into the southern port of Kinsale. The English defeated the invaders and the Ulstermen who attempted to join them. Leading Ulster aristocrats, now defeated, abandoned their land for European exile. The 'plantation' programme continued fitfully. During the reign of James I, most of the northern land was confiscated and 'planted' with thousands of Scots and English, who changed the face of the province. After the English Civil War, Oliver Cromwell, England's ruler, ruthlessly massacred the garrisons at Drogheda and Wexford as the price for their support of Charles I, and pursued his own colonisation of Ireland. From 1654, Catholics were only allowed to hold land west of the River Shannon, much of it scarcely habitable. 'To Hell or Connaught' was the slogan used to sum up the alternatives for the dispossessed.

After the religious war that culminated in the Battle of the Boyne *(see below)*, the Irish Catholic majority was subjected to further persecution in the form of the Penal Laws, introduced by the all-Protestant Irish parliament and designed to keep Catholics away from positions of power and influence.

Revolutionary Ideas

It took the American Revolution to provoke daring new thinking in Ireland. Henry Grattan led agitation for greater freedom and tolerance. A Protestant of aristocratic heritage, he staunchly defended in the House of Commons in London the rights of all Irishmen. Further pressure came from an Irish Protestant, Theobald Wolfe Tone, a young lawyer campaigning for parliamentary reform and the abolition of anti-Catholic laws. In 1793 Catholics won the vote and other concessions for which Tone fought. Five years later, with the United Irishmen in rebellion, a French squadron came to their aid off the coast of Donegal. It was swiftly intercepted by British naval forces and

---

Battle of the Boyne

Ireland became the battleground for an English power struggle when William of Orange, a Dutchman and a Protestant, challenged his father-in-law, the Catholic James II, for the British throne. From exile in France, James sailed to Ireland to mobilise allies and met William's army in July 1690 at the River Boyne. The Orangemen, aided by troops from several Protestant countries, vastly outnumbered the Irish and French forces. As battles go, it set no records for scope or tactical innovation. But the anniversary of William's victory is still celebrated with fervour by Protestants in Northern Ireland.

> Daniel O'Connell tried to gain the repeal of the Act of Union , and although he failed, he is still remembered in Ireland as 'the Liberator'.

Wolfe Tone was captured on board the flagship. Convicted of treason, he cut his own throat before his sentence of death by hanging could be carried out.

In 1801 the Irish Parliament voted itself out of business by approving the Act of Union which established the United Kingdom of Great Britain and Ireland. To help shape a common economic and political destiny for the two islands, all Irish MPs would now sit at Westminster. In 1823 Daniel O'Connell founded the Catholic Association to work for emancipation. Five years later, he won a landslide victory for the House of Commons, but as a Catholic was legally forbidden to take it. To prevent conflict, Parliament passed the Emancipation Act (1829), removing the most discriminatory laws.

Starvation and Emigration

One of the worst disasters of 19th-century Europe was the great Irish famine. The problem emerged in September 1845, when potato blight was found on farms in southeast Ireland. The British government set up an investigation, but the outbreak was mis-diagnosed. The next crop failed nationwide, wiping out the staple food of the Irish peasant. Cruel winter weather and the outbreak of disease added to the horror of starvation. Believing that they should not interfere with free market forces, the British government did not provide relief.

Survivors fled the stricken land aboard creaking 'coffin ships'. Irish refugees swamped towns such as Liverpool, Halifax, Boston and New York. The famine reduced the population of Ireland by two million – half dying, the rest emigrating. It took another century for the decline in population figures to be reversed and the flow of emigrants stemmed.

Frustration and Revolt

At the end of the 19th century Nationalist sentiment was encouraged, and manifested itself in the formation of such groups as the Gaelic Athletic Association and the Gaelic League. In 1905 a number of nationalist groups were consolidated in a movement called Sinn Féin ('We Ourselves').

As Britain entered World War I, activists planned an opportunistic revolt. In the Easter Rising of 1916 rebels seized the General Post Office in Dublin and declared Ireland's independence from Britain. The authorities crushed the rising, which had lacked widespread support, but their pitiless execution of the ringleaders reversed public opinion. The war of independence had, in effect, begun.

Emigration statue in County Cork

At the next general election the nationalist Sinn Féin, led by Eamon de Valera, won by a landslide. The newly elected Sinn Féin parliamentarians refused to fill their posts in the Commons in London, but set themselves up in Dublin as Dáil Éireann, the new parliament of Ireland.

More than two years of guerrilla warfare followed until the partition of Ireland was agreed in December 1921. Under it, six counties of the north, where the Protestant majority refused to accept rule from Dublin, were allowed to remain part of the United Kingdom. The other 26 counties had a Catholic majority and became the Irish Free State (Éire), a dominion within the British Empire. The British optimistically predicted that the two sides would soon patch up their differences and that the border would be dissolved amicably. But many republicans refused to accept the settlement and a bitter civil war broke out in the South. The war ended in 1923 with the effective surrender of Eamon de Valera's anti-treaty forces, though he himself was to come to power nine years later, vowing to reinstate the ancient Gaelic language and culture. The 26 counties remained neutral in World War II and formally became an independent republic in 1949.

Britain left Northern Ireland to its own devices and its own government. Many Catholics would not recognise the province's legitimacy, and many Protestants responded by ensuring that the all-too-scarce jobs and public housing went mainly to Protestants. In 1969 civil rights marches against these injustices were repressed, unleashing old hatreds. Terrorism and bitter internecine violence were to last for three decades.

The Good Friday Agreement, signed in 1998, established the framework for a self-governing Northern Ireland with power sharing. But many Protestant politicians refused to cooperate with their nationalist counterparts until the Irish Republican Army disarmed completely. Periods of partial self-rule alternated with direct rule from Britain, as a compromise was sought. Compromise, though, was a flower that had never taken root easily in Irish soil.

Mary McAleese, Ireland's second woman president in a row

Historical Landmarks

c. 7000 BC Date of earliest archaeological evidence along the coast.

c. 500 BC Celts migrate to Britain. Ireland's Iron Age begins.

c. 432 St Patrick returns to Ireland as a missionary.

1014 Brian Ború, High King of Ireland, defeats Vikings near Clontarf.

1366 Statutes of Kilkenny forbid English to intermarry or speak Gaelic.

1541 Henry VIII declares himself King of Ireland.

1607 The most powerful Irish princes flee to Spain (Flight of the Earls).

1608 James I moves Protestant Scots and English to Ulster Plantation.

1649 Oliver Cromwell conquers Ireland in a merciless campaign.

1690 William of Orange defeats England's Catholic King James II at the Battle of the Boyne. The 'Protestant Ascendancy' begins.

1800 Act of Union makes Ireland part of the United Kingdom.

1845–51 The Great Potato Famine deprives one-third of the Irish population of their main source of nutrition. Over 1 million people die.

1905 Sinn Féin ('We Ourselves') is formed 'to make England take one hand from Ireland's throat and the other out of Ireland's pocket'.

1916 James Connolly and Pádraig Pearse lead 1,800 volunteers who occupy public buildings in the 'Easter Rising'. Britain's harsh response strengthens the nationalists' cause.

1918–23 Sinn Féin wins a landslide of seats in parliament and announces formation of Irish parliament in Dublin. After the 1919–21 Anglo-Irish War, the treaty creates the Irish Free State, excluding the six counties of Northern Ireland with Protestant majorities.

1937 The Free State, Éire, adopts its own constitution.

1949 Having remained neutral in World War II, Éire leaves the British Commonwealth and becomes the Republic of Ireland.

1972 British soldiers shoot dead 13 demonstrators on 'Bloody Sunday'. Belfast's parliament is dissolved. Northern Ireland is ruled from London.

1973 The Republic of Ireland joins the EEC (now the European Union).

1998 The Good Friday Agreement is signed in Northern Ireland.

2002 The Republic of Ireland adopts the euro.

2003 Fresh elections for the Northern Ireland Assembly are held.

WHERE TO GO

The best way to see Ireland is by car, though various package deals or bus tours exist as an alternative. You can see a good deal of the country using public transport, although apart from the main routes, the bus schedules are designed more for country folk than tourists.

This book covers the highlights of the Republic and Northern Ireland, starting in Dublin and proceeding more or less clockwise. We cannot describe all the sights – or even all the counties – but wherever you go, you'll enjoy Ireland best at an unhurried Irish pace.

DUBLIN

The Republic of Ireland's capital (pop. over 1.5 million) is the birthplace and inspiration of many great authors, and an elegant European city with many outstanding examples of 18th-century architecture. Dublin is pervaded by contrasting moods; from its noble avenues and intimate side streets to chic shopping and old smoky pubs, there are also museums, colleges and plenty of sports. In this melting pot of old and new, traditional lace still masks modern windows.

O'Connell Street to St Stephen's Green

The main avenue in Dublin is **O'Connell Street**. Measuring 46m (150ft) across, it has five monuments to Irish history lined along the middle. The most recent is the Millennium Spike, replacing the 19th-century Nelson Pillar blown up in 1966 in an act of defiance against the British.

O'Connell Street's most famous landmark is the **General Post Office**. The GPO was the command post of the 1916

Dunguaire Castle, built in 1520 at Kinvara in the Far West

The Custom House dominates the north bank of the river

Easter Rising and was badly damaged in the fighting. A plaque on the front of the building and paintings inside mark the event.

Just opposite O'Connell Bridge is the imposing monument honouring 'The Liberator', Daniel O'Connell (1775–1847, *see page 18*), after whom both the street and bridge are named.

From the bridge, almost as wide as it is long, you can look up and down the **River Liffey** and along the embankments. To the east, beyond the skyscraper-style headquarters of the Irish trade union movement, rises the copper dome of the 18th-century **Custom House**. Like many buildings along the Liffey, it was all but destroyed in the civil war of 1921, but has now been restored. To the west is the **Ha'penny Bridge**, so called because that's what it originally cost to cross it.

The momentous white building facing College Green on the south side of the River Liffey is a branch of the **Bank of Ireland**, but its grandeur derivedfrom its original purpose of housing parliament in the 18th century, the bank moved in when parliament was abolished by the Act of Union in 1801 *(see page 18)*. The **Bank of Ireland Arts Centre**, just behind it, holds lunch-time and evening concerts and exhibitions.

Behind the railings at the entrance to **Trinity College** are the statues of two famous alumni – philosopher Edmund Burke and playwright Oliver Goldsmith. Founded by Queen Elizabeth I in 1592, Trinity is a timeless enclave of calm and scholarship in the middle of this bustling city. For centuries it was seen as an exclusively Protestant institution, and as recently as 1956 the Catholic church forbade its students to attend Trinity 'under pain of mortal sin'. Today, TCD, as it is called, is integrated. Students lead informative, bargain-priced college tours from a kiosk near the entrance.

The campus forms a monument to the good taste of the 18th century, and visitors enjoy cobbled walks amongst trimmed lawns, fine old trees, statues and stone buildings. You can also enjoy the Dublin Experience here, an audio-visual show of the city's history and the art exhibitions on show at the Douglas Hyde Gallery.

The greatest treasures are in the vaulted Long Room in the **Old Library** (open Mon–Sat 9.30am–5pm, Sun noon–4.30pm, 9.30am–4.30pm in summer), where double-decker shelving holds thousands of books published prior to 1800,

Trinity College Old Library

and priceless early manuscripts are displayed in glass cases. In the adjacent Colonnades Gallery, queues of tourists reverently wait for a look at the **Book of Kells**. This 340-page parchment wonder, handwritten and illustrated by monks during the 9th century, contains a Latin version of the New Testament. The beauty of the script – the illumination (the decoration of initial letters and words) – and the bright abstract designs make this the most wonderful treasure to survive from Ireland's Golden Age. The vellum leaves are turned every day to protect them from light and to give visitors a chance to come back for more.

A left turn on leaving Trinity by the main gate brings you to the entrance of **Grafton Street**, the main shopping and social artery of the city's southside. More than anywhere else, Grafton Street exudes a sense of Dublin's knack for seeming to bustle and dawdle at the same time. Bewley's first Oriental Café is the street's traditional hub. Though the food is unremarkable, the coffee and sticky buns are great and the atmosphere unique.

Examples of Europe's finest Georgian houses can be seen facing **Merrion Square**. The discreet, smart brick houses have Georgian doorways flanked by tall columns and topped by fanlights. No two are alike. In a complex of formal buildings on the west side of the square stands the city's largest 18th-century mansion, home of the Duke of Leinster. Today **Leinster House** is the seat of the Irish parliament, which consists of the Senate *(Seanad Éireann)* and the Chamber of Deputies (the *Dáil*, pronounced 'doyle'); and just north of here on Merrion Square West is the National Gallery.

Standing at the entrance to the **National Gallery** (open Mon–Sat 9.30am–5.30pm, Sun noon–5.30pm) you will see a statue of George Bernard Shaw, famous and respected Dubliner known locally as a benefactor of the institution. In the gallery, some 2,000 works of art are displayed. Irish

This stylish commercial centre is on Grafton Street, the city's main shopping thoroughfare

artists receive priority, but other nationalities are well represented, such as Dutch, English, Flemish, French, Italian and Spanish masters. Among those on display are Fra' Angelico, Rubens, Rembrandt, Canaletto, Gainsborough and Goya. In addition, there are two treasured frescoes dating from the 11th or 12th centuries.

The main entrance to the **National Museum** (open Tues–Sat 10am–5pm, Sun 2–5pm), a Dublin institution, is reached from Kildare Street. The museum's collection of Irish antiquities contains several surprises, from old skeletons and tools to exquisite gold ornaments of the Bronze Age. The most famous items on display include the 8th-century Ardagh Chalice, the delicate Tara Brooch from the same era and the 12th-century Shrine of St Patrick's Bell. You can also see ancient Ogham stones and admire many replicas of the greatest carved stone crosses from the early centuries of Christian Ireland.

The city's name comes from the Irish Dubhlinn, meaning 'a dark pool', and a much older Gaelic name on buses and signs – Baile Atha Cliath, 'the town of the hurdle ford'.

Dublin is well-endowed with squares and parks. The biggest of these – and possibly the biggest city square in Europe – is the famous **St Stephen's Green**. During the 18th century the square was almost completely surrounded by elegant town houses. Some survive today, though many conservationists despair at the rapidly declining number. Inside the square is a delightful park with flower gardens and an artificial lake favoured by waterfowl. Among many sculptures and monuments is a memorial to the poet and playwright W.B. Yeats by Henry Moore. Nearby is also a bust to commemorate Yeats's friend, the Countess Constance Markievicz, who defended the square during the 1916 insurrection, and who was the first woman elected to the British House of Commons (although she declined to take her seat, preferring the Dáil).

Another statue honours the man who paid for landscaping the square: Lord Ardilaun, son of the founder of the Guinness brewery. Some thirsty sightseers might be inspired to find a nearby pub and raise a toast to the stout-hearted benefactor.

Medieval Dublin

Dublin Castle (open Mon–Fri 10am–5pm, Sat and Sun 2–5pm) was begun in the 13th century, set on a hill above the original Viking settlement on the south bank of the River Liffey, but was mostly rebuilt during the 18th century. Over the years it has served as a seat of government, a prison, a courthouse, and occasionally as a fortress under siege. Many visiting heads of state have stayed in the lavish State Apartments.

Just behind the castle is the **Chester Beatty Library** (open Mon–Fri 10am–5pm, Sat 11am–5pm, Sun 1–5pm; closed Mon

Oct–Apr), a collection of priceless manuscripts and miniatures from the East: jade books from China, early Arabic tomes on geography and astronomy, and a sampling of Korans. Around the corner from the castle stands **City Hall**, built during the late 18th century in solid, classical style. Downstairs is an exhibition detailing the story of the Irish capital.

Dublin has two noteworthy cathedrals to offer, and although it is the official capital of what is a predominantly Catholic country, both belong to the Protestant Church of Ireland.

Christ Church Cathedral (open Mon–Fri 9.45am–5pm, Sat and Sun 10am–5pm) is the older of the two, dating from 1038. One unusual architectural touch is the covered pedestrian bridge over Winetavern Street, which links the church and its Synod Hall. This was built during the Victorian era, but doesn't spoil the overall mood. Otherwise, the cathedral contains Romanesque as well as Early English and fine Neo-Gothic elements.

Christ Church Cathedral

If you would like to delve more deeply into Irish history, you could visit the Synod Hall to see **Dublinia** (open Apr–Sept: daily 10am–5pm; Oct–Mar: Mon–Sat 11am–4pm, Sun 10am–4.30pm). This is an impressive multimedia heritage centre depicting how Dubliners lived in the medieval city, offering Viking artefacts and a closing audiovisual show.

The crypt, now displaying many of Christ Church's more valuable treasures, runs under the full length of the church, and is a surviving remnant from the 12th century, during which time the cathedral was expanded by Strongbow *(see page 15)*, whose mortal remains lie buried here. Although it has been regarded as authentic for many decades, modern scholars are in heated debate about the authenticity of the Strongbow tomb. You can see the fine statue of a recumbent cross-legged knight in full armour upstairs.

A short walk south from Christ Church Cathedral leads to Dublin's newer and larger cathedral, **St Patrick's** (open Mar–Oct: Mon–Sat 9am–6pm, Sun 9–11am, 12.45–3pm and 4.15–6pm; Nov–Feb: Mon–Fri 9am–6pm, Sat 9am–5pm, Sun 10–11am and 12.45–3pm), which is dedicated to Ireland's national saint. It is said that St Patrick himself baptised 5th-century converts at a well on this very site; indeed, a stone slab used for covering the well can be found in the northwest

Temple Bar

Temple Bar is a network of small streets full of studios, galleries, second-hand bookshops, clothing outlets and music stores. There are countless restaurants, pubs and crafts shops. Many Dubliners regard it as a tourist trap, but it has some worthwhile cultural centres.

Arthouse: the world's first purpose-built multimedia centre for the arts.
Temple Bar Music Centre: workshop and venue for concerts.
Irish Film Centre: arthouse cinema with bookshop, cafe/restaurant, bar and film archive.
Gallery of Photography: exhibits Irish and international work.
National Photographic Archive: maintains and exhibits historical images of Ireland.
DESIGNyard: applied arts centre displaying and selling Irish jewellery.
The Ark: a cultural centre for children.

Getting floored with the locals in Temple Bar

of the cathedral. This church was consecrated in 1192, but the present structure dates mostly from the 13th and 14th centuries. The cathedral is known for its association with Jonathan Swift, author of *Gulliver's Travels*, who was appointed dean in 1713 and served until his death in 1745. Many Swiftian relics can be seen in a corner of the north transept, and a simple brass plate in the floor near the entrance marks his grave. Next to this you can see the tomb of the mysterious Stella, one of the two great loves of his life. Above the lintel of the robing room you can read his own bitter epitaph, written in Latin: 'Savage indignation can no longer gnaw his heart. Go, traveller, and imitate, if you can, this earnest and dedicated defender of liberty'.

The talented choirboys of St Patrick's Cathedral sing at the services given every day of the week except Saturdays. A joint choir formed from both cathedrals was the first to sing Handel's *Messiah* when the composer was in Dublin in 1742. A copy from the year 1799 can be seen in **Marsh's Library**

Rotten luck at St Michan's

(open daily except Tues and Thur 10am–1pm and 2–5pm, Sat 10.30am–1pm), Ireland's first public library, founded in 1701.

Called the 'Left Bank' by tourist officials, **Temple Bar** *(see page 30)* is Dublin's cultural quarter, running from Westmoreland Street to Christ Church Cathedral. With its 18th- and 19th-century architecture it's not just the arts and crafts quarter of Dublin, but also a land of themed bars and raucous nightclubs. The area is worth visiting, but select your culture carefully.

The North Bank

The most impressive building located on the north bank of the Liffey is the domed home of the **Four Courts** (originally the Chancery, Common Pleas, Exchequer and King's Bench). This is the magnificent work of James Gandon, the respected 18th-century English-born architect who also designed Dublin's Custom House. The courthouse was seriously damaged by the consistent and prolonged shelling during the 1922 civil war. After lengthy reconstruction, however, it was restored, and justice continues to be dispensed in the Four Courts. Carrying on the tradition introduced by the British, Irish lawyers wear wigs and gowns when in Superior Courts.

St Michan's Church (open Mar–Oct: Mon–Fri 10am–12.45pm and 2–4.45pm, Sat 10am–12.45pm; Nov–Mar:

Mon–Fri 12.30–3.30pm, Sat 10am–12.45pm) just around the corner in Church Street, was founded in 1095 but has been rebuilt on several occasions since. Among the curiosities is an unusual 'Penitent's Pew', in which sinners had to sit and confess their sins aloud to the whole congregation. In the crypt, wood coffins and mummies can be seen in a remarkable state of preservation. Some of them have been here for about 800 years, saved from deterioration by the dry atmosphere. You can touch the finger of the mummified crusader for good luck.

The last imposing official building to be designed by the architect James Gandon was the **King's Inns**, which houses the headquarters of the Irish legal profession. It contains an important law library and a magnificent dining hall, where grand portraits of many judges decorate the walls.

On the north side of Parnell Square is Charlemont House, an attractive 18th-century mansion which is now the **Hugh Lane Municipal Gallery of Modern Art** (open Tues–Thur 9.30am–6pm, Fri–Sat 9.30am–5pm, Sun 11am–5pm). It includes works from the fine collection of Sir Hugh Lane, whose drowning in the *Lusitania* disaster of 1915 *(see page 56)* provoked a long legal battle over custody of his paintings. The current agreement assures the Municipal Gallery three-quarters of the contested legacy, including works by Corot, Courbet, Manet, Monet and Rousseau. The gallery also houses the Francis Bacon Studio, its contents transported from London in 1998 and meticulously recreated, along with displays of the famous artist's works.

Two literary attractions are nearby. **The Dublin Writers Museum** (open Mon–Sat 10am–5pm, Sun 11am–5pm), just next door to the gallery, displays photographs, busts, manuscripts and first editions relating to writers such as Swift, Shaw, Yeats, O'Casey, Joyce, Beckett and Behan. At No 35 Great George's Street is the **James Joyce Centre** (open Mon–Sat 9.30am–5pm, Sun 12.30–5pm), aimed at Joyce enthusiasts.

An evening stroll in Phoenix Park

Beyond the Centre

Phoenix Park provides Dubliners with nearly 3 sq miles (8 sq km) of beautiful parkland. Its huge monument is an obelisk honouring the Duke of Wellington, who was born in Ireland but played down his Irishness, quipping that although a man may be born in a stable, that wouldn't make him a horse. Among the buildings discreetly located in the park are the residence of the President of Ireland (*Áras an Uachtaráin*) and the Ashtown Castle Heritage Centre, which details the history of the park and its flora and fauna. On the northeast side of the park, Dublin **zoo** provides education and diversion; it is noted for breeding lion cubs in captivity.

In Kilmainham on the South Circular Road, a stone tower gate guards the grounds of the **Royal Hospital**, which was a home for army pensioners. Now it is the **Irish Museum of Modern Art** (open Tues–Sat 10am–5.30pm, Sun noon–5.30pm) and holds first-class temporary exhibitions.

The ugly and forbidding **Kilmainham Gaol** (open daily 9.30am–4.45pm; closed Sat Oct–Mar) has been restored as if it were a work of art. The prisoners who lived and died within its walls include many of the heroes of Irish nationalism. The central cell-block shows exhibits from Ireland's stormy history.

Many make their way to the city's biggest commercial enterprise, the **Guinness Brewery** (open Tues–Sat 9.30am–5pm, Sun 10.30am–4pm), at St James' Gate since 1759. Its dark, full-bodied stout is world-renowned. Visitors to its award winning **Storehouse** get an entertaining explanation of how the brew is made and a sample of the finished product.

DUBLIN DAYTRIPS

North of Dublin

In the northeastern part of the Bay, **Howth peninsula** makes an appealing starting point for those wishing to venture out of Dublin. From the vantage point of the 170-m (560-ft) Hill of Howth, you can survey the bay and the open sea. Howth Harbour, on the north side of the peninsula, is a fishing port and haven for pleasure boats. From here you can see and visit Ireland's Eye, an islet 1.5km (1 mile) offshore that is popular with birds and bird-watchers.

Malahide, a small resort town, is best known for its **castle** (open Mon–Fri 10am–5pm, Sat–Sun 11am–6pm), a two-turreted medieval pile. The spirit of the Talbot family, who resided here for 791 years, still pervades. Part of the National Portrait Collection is housed here and well-kept

Malahide Castle

lawns surround the castle. Nearby, the **Fry Model Railway Museum** (open Mon–Thur 10am–6pm, Sat 11am–6pm, Sun 2–6pm; weekends 2–5pm Oct–Mar) is the largest model railway in Ireland and one of the largest in Europe. It shows transport in Ireland dating back more than 150 years, and all of it is electronically controlled.

Drogheda, a small industrial town, straddles the River Boyne near the site of the 1690 battle in which King James II missed his chance to recover the English crown *(see page 17)*. This medieval city was surrounded by a wall with 10 gates – you can still drive through the 13th-century **St Lawrence's Gate**, with its two towers standing as vigilantly as ever.

The head of the martyred Oliver Plunkett, St Peter's

In the town centre **St Peter's Church** has been dedicated to St Oliver Plunkett (1628–81), the Archbishop of Armagh, who was executed by the British in connection with an alleged papist plot. Several relics of the local saint are displayed in the church, including the actual door of his cell at Newgate Prison and, most amazing of all, his head, which is embalmed and kept in a gold case in a side altar.

About 10km (6 miles) to the northwest is **Monasterboice** (St Buite's Abbey), one of Ireland's numerous ancient monastic settlements. Over it stands the jagged top of what is thought to have been the tallest round tower in Ireland, 34m (110ft) high. Along with the remains of two ruined churches there are three important examples of early Christian high crosses, with intricately carved figures.

A high medieval gatehouse guards the approach to **Mellifont Abbey** (open May–Oct: daily 10am–6pm), Ireland's most important early Cistercian monastery. Among the buildings stand the remains of a large church and the Lavabo, a graceful octagonal building of which only four sides remain today. Like other abandoned monastic institutions, Mellifont is set in peaceful and verdant country.

The overwhelming demand to see Newgrange during the winter solstice has forced Irish Heritage to hold a lottery. Visitors can sign up in the welcome centre. Or you can telephone them on 041 988 0300 and they'll enter your name.

Newgrange (Brú na Boinne Visitor Centre; open daily, Mar–Apr 9.30am–5.30pm, May: 9am–6.30pm, Jun–Sept 9am–7pm, Oct 9.30am–5.30pm, Nov–Feb 9am–5pm), a large Neolithic tomb in the Boyne Valley, looks like a man-made hilltop, but is in fact an amazing feat of prehistoric engineering – one of Europe's best examples of a passage-grave. The narrow tunnel leading to the central shrine is positioned to let the sun shine in precisely on the shortest day of the year, 21 December. The 19-m (62-ft) tunnel is just high and wide enough for you to walk through at a crouch. At the end of it you can stand in the circular vault and look up at the ceiling to see the remarkable 4,000-year-old technique used in its construction.

Intriguing carvings in spiral, circular and diamond designs decorate the stones in the inner sanctum and at the entrance. Outside, a dozen large, upright stones, about a third of those originally placed here, form a protective circle around the mound. There is an extensive heritage centre at the site. Two

The sacred mound at Newgrange

further Neolithic tumuli, at Knowth and Dowth, suggest that this was regarded as a special place in prehistoric times.

The scribes and artists of the monastery at **Kells**, in County Meath, produced the nation's most beautiful book, now on display at Trinity College in Dublin *(see page 26)*. The town of Kells has grown up around the monastic settlement, and there is a fine Celtic cross standing at the main traffic junction. Near the cemetery are several other stone crosses and a round tower.

As its name indicates, **Trim** is a well-kept, tidy town, but the English name is derived from the Irish *Baile Atha Trium*, which means 'the town of the Elder Tree Ford'. Trim claims it has Ireland's largest medieval **castle** (open daily 10am–6pm), once a Norman stronghold. Vast it is, but time has left only the bare bones. The Dublin Gate in the south once contained a prison. On the opposite side of the river, the Yellow Steeple was part of a Augustinian abbey established in the 13th century; the tower was blown up to keep it out of the hands of Cromwell.

West of Dublin

County Kildare has some of the greenest pastures in all of Ireland. It's a great area for sports, and there are plenty of historic sites amidst the rolling hills. **Maynooth**, a pleasant town with an historic college and the ruins of a 12th-century castle, is a training centre for priests. Founded in 1795, **St Patrick's College** is seen as one of the foremost Catholic seminaries in the world.

On the edge of Celbridge village, **Castletown House** (guided tours only, Mon–Fri 10am–6pm, Sat–Sun 1–6pm) stands at the end of a long avenue of trees. This stately home, in Palladian style, was erected in 1722 for the speaker of the Irish House of Commons, William Connolly, and has been re-stored and refurnished with 18th-century antiques and paintings. About 5km (3 miles) from the house, Connolly's widow ordered the construction of a monstrous obelisk. Known as Connolly's Folly, it was erected to provide jobs for local workers suffering from the Great Famine of the 1740s.

The administrative centre of the county, **Naas** (the Irish *Nas na Riogh*, means 'Assembly Place of the Kings') has an important racecourse. So does nearby Punchestown, but the capital of horse racing and breeding is the **Curragh**, a prairie extending all the way from Droichead Nua (New Bridge) to Kildare Town. It's a shock to come upon a modern grandstand – site of the Irish Sweeps Derby – in the middle of this vast plain.

Many winners of the biggest races are born at the **National Stud Farm** at Tully (open Feb–Nov: daily

> The ruins of an ancient monastery are at the southern end of County Kildare, in the village of Castledermot. Two beautifully carved crosses remain near the portal of a church that could be as much as a thousand years old. The design of this ruin is repeated in a new church just a few yards behind it.

The Japanese Gardens in Kildare

9.30am–6pm). Here thoroughbreds live in a first-class 'horse resort'. Beside the Irish Horse Museum, there is an immaculate **Japanese Garden**. At the beginning of the 20th century, a Japanese gardener and 40 locals spent four years changing a bog into a world of tidy shrubs and disciplined trees. There's even a lotus pond, teahouse and red wooden bridge.

The town of **Kildare** is also remembered for the double monastery (monks and nuns) founded there by 5th-century St Brigid. Though Vikings and other invaders damaged the buildings quite badly, the shape of the 19th-century **cathedral** features 13th-century elements. Nearby you can inspect an ancient round tower still in very good shape, with stairs all the way to the summit.

South of Dublin

Dún Laoghaire (pronounced Dunleary), just south of Dublin, is Ireland's leading yachting centre and a car ferry terminal. The piers at the harbour are 2km (1 mile) long, leaving plenty of space between for the huge fleet of pleasure boats that dock here. Construction of the harbour was a great feat of 19th-century engineering – and is still impressive. You can also visit the Maritime Museum (closed for restoration until autumn 2004), featuring exhibits relating to Ireland's maritime history.

Around 1.5 km (1 mile) to the south at **Sandycove** is an 18th-century tower. James Joyce lived in it, and used this experience in the opening of his work *Ulysses*. The Martello Tower (named after a Corsican headland with a fort) was part of the coastal defenses built to keep Napoleon at bay. It has been turned into a museum dedicated to Joyce, the **James Joyce Tower and Museum** (open Apr–Oct: Mon–Sat 10am–5pm, Sun 2–6pm). A second Martello Tower can be seen on Dalkey Island, the largest of a group of islands off Dalkey.

Just across the border in County Wicklow, the popular resort of **Bray** has a 2-km (1-mile) sand-and-shingle beach backed by an esplanade. The Wicklow coast is mostly sandy and low-lying, and the interior of the county is known as the Garden of Ireland.

West of Bray, near the small village of Enniskerry, is the grand estate of **Powerscourt** (house and grounds open daily 9.30am–sunset). Covering 20 hectares (47 acres) of glorious countryside and gardens, the estate has an 18th-century, 100-room mansion at its centre, which was damaged in a fire in 1974. Today it contains an exhibition devoted to the history of the estate. From the house, disciplined terraces descend to a lake with a fountain in the middle. The garden centre is also worth a visit, as is the Powerscourt Waterfall, 5km (3 miles) south of the house.

Powerscourt House and Gardens

In a narrow, wooded valley with two lakes stand the evocative ruins of the ancient monastic settlement of **Glendalough** (open Oct–Mar: daily 9.30am–5pm;

Apr–Nov: 9.30am–6pm). The hermit St Kevin founded the monastery here in the 6th century, evidently inspired by the breathtaking scenery and the remoteness of the locale. He planned it as a small, contemplative institution, but as its fame spread far and wide, Glendalough of the Seven Churches became an important monastic centre, until 1398, when it was destroyed by Anglo-Normans.

The buildings which survive date from the 8th and 12th centuries. The most famous is the **round tower**, which is 34m (112ft) high and 16m (52ft) in circumference at the base. This was the place to sit out any sieges; its doorway is built 3.5m (11ft) above the ground – enough to discourage even Vikings from invading. Remnants of a cathedral, stone churches and decorated crosses can also be seen, and the original gateway to the settlement, the only one of its kind in Ireland, is still standing. Inside, on the right, a cross-inscribed stone may have marked the limit of the sanctuary granted to those who took refuge within the monastery. In the graveyard, tombstones dating back hundreds of years sit next to more recent graves.

In **Avondale**, you can visit **Avondale House** (open daily 11am–6pm), the home of Charles Stewart Parnell, the great 19th-century Irish leader, which has been restored in 1850s style. It is set in an area of verdant forest and woodland and

The Wicklow Way

You'll need the better part of a week to see all of this ancient path, which stretches 132km (82 miles) from the suburbs of Dublin to the Wexford border town of Clonegal. A shorter option is the popular stretch from Knockree, 5km (3 miles) west of Enniskerry, to Glendalough. It'll take you about three days to cover this area, and you'll be able to step foot on the highest point of the trail – White Hill, from which on a clear day you can see the mountains in Wales.

makes an ideal destination for walkers. Grand **Russborough House** (open Apr and Oct: Sun and bank hols 10.30am–5.30pm; Jun–Aug: daily 10.30am–5.30pm; May and Sept: Mon–Sat 10.30am–2.30pm), near Blessington, is an 18th-century manor in Palladian style. Today it houses the Sir Alfred Beit Art Collection, and is beautifully and richly decorated, offering magnificent views across the ornamental lake towards the splendid Wicklow mountains.

THE SOUTHEAST

Over the whole year, the southeast enjoys up to an hour more sunshine a day than other parts of Ireland. The better to see – and enjoy – the varied mountains and pastures, rivers, beautiful beaches and delightful old towns.

Enniscorthy (the Irish *Inis Coirthe* means Rock Island) is a colourful inland port on the River Slaney, navigable from

An early high cross at the Irish National Heritage Park *(see page 44)*

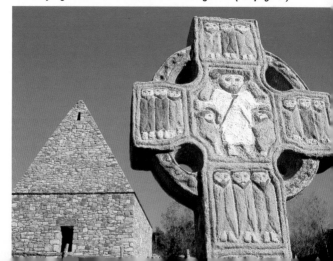

> In the 9th century Wexford was called *Waesfjord*, meaning 'the harbour of the mud-flats'. At low tide, when the bay empties like a sink, the original name still seems appropriate.

here to Wexford. High above the steep streets of the town, Vinegar Hill is a good vantage point for viewing the countryside. It was the scene of the last battle of the 1798 Rising, during which British General Lake overwhelmed the Wexford rebels armed with pitchforks and pikes. **Enniscorthy Castle**, set in the centre of town, is a Norman keep rebuilt during the 16th century and recently opened as the County Wexford Historical and Folk Museum.

Wexford

Wexford, the county seat, 24km (15 miles) to the south, was one of the first Viking settlements. A few ancient monuments survive and are well signposted, with informative plaques explaining almost every local legend. All remaining medieval walls have been restored and a heritage centre has opened.

The **Irish National Heritage Park** (open daily 9.30am–6.30pm) in Ferrycarrig, north of town, contains a collection of lifesize replicas of ancient dwellings, burial sites, old monastic settlements and various types of fortification, from early Irish man to the 12th century. Reminders of the area's seafaring past are on view at the **Maritime Museum**, housed in an old lightship, moored permanently in the harbour of the picturesque village of Kilmore Quay, about 25km (15 miles) south of Wexford.

In October, the Wexford Opera Festival attracts world performers and fans for even little-known works. Southeast of the town, the resort of **Rosslare** has a 10-km (6-mile) crescent of beach. At Rosslare Harbour, car ferries arrive from and depart for Fishguard, Le Havre and Cherbourg.

The tip of the **Hook peninsula** has a tall, 700-year-old lighthouse that warns mariners of treacherous rocks and signals the entrance to Waterford harbour. A light has been kept burning at Hook Head for the past 1,500 years.

The Norse established ports such as Dublin and Wexford, but it somehow never occurred to them to found permanent settlements inland. It was the Normans who moved 32km (20 miles) up the estuary to build the town of **New Ross**, still an important inland port. In the middle of the 13th century, it was encircled by a strong and defensive wall.

The isolated hamlet of **Dunganstown**, near New Ross, was the birthplace of US President John F. Kennedy's great grandfather. A plaque marks the cottage from which he emigrated to Boston. The assassinated president was much admired in Ireland and a group of Irish-Americans and the Irish government later created the **John F. Kennedy Park**, above Dunganstown.

Waterford crystal

Waterford

Waterford is a busy little port situated just 29km (18 miles) from the open sea. From the far side of the River Suir, its long quayside presents a pretty image. The town's foundation can be traced back to the 9th century, but it did not gain its first charter until 1205, granted by King John. The heritage centre has modern audiovisual displays and ancient relics from the Norse and Norman settlements of the city. Municipal mementos, including Waterford's important collection of medieval charters, are preserved inside **Reginald's Tower**, the city's most venerable building, now the civic museum (open daily 9.30am–6.30pm). The walls of this massive circular fortification, 3m (10ft) thick and about 24m (80ft) tall, have survived many sieges since they went up in 1003.

Among other attractions are the Garter Lane Arts Centre, perhaps the country's leading regional centre of its kind. An elegant Georgian street, the Mall, begins at the Quay. Waterford City Hall, built in the 1780s, has many fine features, including two small theatres and a Council Chamber illuminated by a splendid chandelier made from **Waterford glass**.

The golden age of Waterford glass ran from 1783 to 1851. After a century's lapse, production resumed, and the traditional processes can be seen on guided tours of the factory, about 5km (3 miles) from Waterford town centre (open Nov–Feb: daily 9am–5pm; Mar–Oct: 8.30am–6pm).

At the western edge of the county, the **Lismore Experience**, another educational multimedia show, tells the history of this small town founded in the 7th century by St Carthage. Also, **Ormond Castle** in Carrick-on-Suir is a fine example of an old Elizabethan manor, now restored to its 16th-century glory.

Counties **Kilkenny** and **Tipperary** both feature stunning scenery and imposing ruins. Tipperary was home of the kings of Munster; Kilkenny entered history as the ancient Kingdom of Ossory. The main town in County Tipperary is **Clonmel**, where parts of the 14th-century walls can still be seen. The turreted West Gate was rebuilt in 1831 on the site of an original gate. The county museum in Parnell Street is well worth a visit.

The name of the town of **Cahir** is a short version of the Irish for 'Fortress of the Dun Abounding in Fish'. Its setting, on the River Suir, is both attractive and strategic. A seemingly impregnable **castle** (open mid-Mar–mid-Jun: daily 9.30am–5.30pm; June–Sept: 9am–7.30pm; Sept–Oct: 9.30am–5.30pm; Oct–March: 9.30am–4.30pm) guards the crucial crossing. Built on the river's lovely islet – a site fortified since the 3rd century – the present castle dates from the 15th century. It's in a fine state of restoration, and guided tours point out military details, such as musket slits, a portcullis and a cannonball embedded high in one of the walls. While you're in Cahir, take a look at **Swiss Cottage** (open daily 10am–6pm), an early 19th-century cottage, in the bright Regency style. It has been fully restored right down to the thatched roof and original French wallpaper.

Cashel

In **Cashel** (County Tipperary), monastic ruins crown an imposing hilltop. The **Rock of Cashel** (open Mar–Jun: daily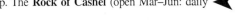

The approach to the Rock of Cashel is a magical experience

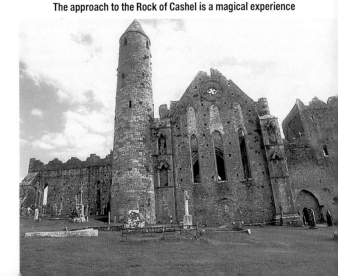

Advice to motorists

9am–5.30pm; Jun–Sept 9am–7.30pm; Sept–Mar 9am–4.30pm), is a 61-m (200-ft) high outcrop of limestone in the middle of a pasture, where the kings of Munster had their headquarters from the 4th to the 12th centuries. When St Patrick visited in 450, he baptised King Aengus and his brothers. In 1101 ecclesiastical authorities built an Irish-Romanesque church on it. **Cormac's Chapel** (consecrated in 1134) is unique in that it was built by Irish monks who interpreted the different architectural styles they had studied in Europe. It features a steeply pitched stone roof, rows of blank arches and two strangely positioned towers. Stone-carvings of beasts and abstract designs decorate the doorway and arches.

The chapel is dwarfed by the **cathedral** which abuts it. This structure, dating from the 13th century, has thick and well-preserved walls, but the roof collapsed during the 18th century. On the positive side, the resulting hole lets the sunlight stream in, helping to clarify the many architectural details, as well as the exquisite medieval stone-carvings.

Inside the entrance, St Patrick's Cross is one of the oldest crosses in Ireland, and it looks like it – the sculptures on both sides are very weatherbeaten. The cross rises up from the 'Coronation Stone', said to have been a pagan sacrificial altar.

It was in the lively market town of **Thurles**, in 1174, that the Irish forces defeated the Anglo-Norman army led by Strongbow *(see page 15)*. Seven hundred years later, the town was to be the birthplace of the Gaelic Athletic Association (GAA), now an amateur sports organisation. The GAA centre offers a multimedia show on the history of Gaelic games. The most conspicuous landmark of the town, the Catholic Cathedral, is a 19th-century impression of the Romanesque style. The square bell tower, 38m (125ft) high, can be seen for miles around.

On the west bank of the River Suir, 6km (4 miles) south of Thurles is the Cistercian **Holy Cross Abbey**. Construction of the church here, which is still in worship, started in Romanesque style, but this slowly evolved into Gothic. The solid white walls, enhanced by window-tracery, reach up to a perfectly restored 15th-century ceiling. Experts acclaim the beautiful sedilia, and the triple-arched recess containing seats of honour carved from jet-black marble and decorated with ancient coats of arms. Another detail is the night stairs, down which the monks stumbled from their sleeping quarters at 2am to chant matins. One of the bells in the tower was cast in the early 13th century, making it Ireland's oldest.

The inner courtyard of Holy Cross Abbey

Enjoying a pint

Kilkenny

Kilkenny has a colourful past and present. Among other surprises, you will find, smack in the traffic-clogged city centre, an enormous medieval castle with acres of lawns – and a river to boot. This was the capital of the old Kingdom of Ossory, a small, feuding realm in pre-Norman Ireland.

Parliament, which convened here in 1366, passed the notorious but ineffectual Statutes of Kilkenny, with the aim of segregating the Irish from the Anglo-Normans; in those days intermarriage was seen as high treason. In the 17th century an independent Irish parliament met here for several years. Oliver Cromwell took the town for the English in 1650, suffering heavy losses in the process.

The Irish *Cill Choinnigh* means St Canice's church. **St Canice's Cathedral**, built in the 13th century, is on the original site of the church which gave the town its name. Though Cromwell's rampaging troops badly damaged the building, it has since been restored to an admirable state. Medieval sculptures and monuments abound in this Protestant church. Alongside it is a round tower, part of the ancient church, so tall, slim and austere that it resembles a factory smokestack.

Kilkenny Castle (open Oct–May: 10.30am–5pm; Jun–Aug: 9.30am–7pm; Sept: 10am–6.30pm) was built in the 13th century to replace the primitive fortress erected by Strongbow. The Butler family, one of the great Anglo-Norman dynasties, held the castle until 1935, but today it is owned by the Irish state. Three of the castle's original four towers remain. You will also find a restored picture gallery on the upper floor of the north wing.

Kilkenny is packed with bright shops. In the High Street, the Tholsel (city hall), dating from the 18th century, has an eight-sided clock tower like a lighthouse. The Archaeological Society in Kilkenny runs a museum in **Rothe House**, a Tudor town house dating from 1594. The exhibits on display range from Stone Age tools unearthed locally to medieval relics.

Not far from **Thomastown** (in County Kilkenny) you can visit the partially restored ruins of the Cistercian **Jerpoint Abbey** (open Mar–May and Sept-Oct: 10am–5pm; Jun–Sept 9.30am–5.30pm; Nov: 10am–4pm). Founded in the mid-12th century by the King of Ossory, it had a brief but troubled history before succumbing to the dissolution of the monasteries in 1540. Parts of the church retain the Romanesque lines, but the square central tower with its stepped battlements was added during the 15th century. Much of the sculptural work in the cloister and the church itself is intact, and you can see larger-than-life carvings of knights and saintly figures, which make inspiring monuments not only to those they honour, but also to the many talented sculptors who worked devotedly at this abbey in the Middle Ages.

Jerpoint Abbey at Thomastown

THE SOUTHWEST

Cork

Ireland's largest county marries gently rolling farmland with rugged, stony peninsulas and delightful bays. Enclosed by steep hills, **Cork City** has all the usual facilities – and traffic jams – of an important commercial and industrial centre, but its atmosphere is unique. The River Lee attracts seagulls, white swans and giant freighters to the centre of town.

The name of the city has nothing to do with trees or bottle-stoppers. Cork, an anglicisation of *Corcaigh*, is translated as 'Marshy Place', which is how the area looked in the 6th century when St Finbarr arrived to found a church and school. In the year 820 the Vikings raided marshy Cork, destroying the institutions and houses. They liked the lay of the land and returned to build their own town on the same site. This destruction and rebuilding was repeated like a pattern in the 17th century and then again during the 'Troubles' of 1919–21.

The main office for Cork and Kerry Tourism is located on the Grand Parade in Cork and offers free maps of the city centre. Cork's beauty begs slow exploration and one can easily spend the day strolling along its narrow canals and winding streets.

Cornmarket Street, Cork

Patrick Street, the wide main street of Cork, is curved because it was built above a river channel. It makes for great window-shopping any-time and is full of people promenading on Saturday af-ternoons. A venture across the south channel of the River Lee will take you to **St Finbarr's Cathedral**. The latest version was built in the 19th century and follows the

A famous place for cosy jumpers

lofty French-Gothic style, with arches upon arches. Across the river's north channel on the Christy Ring Bridge and up the hill is Shandon Church. This distinctive steeple has always been a favourite city landmark. Visitors can climb up through the clockwork intricacies and even play a tune on the bells.

Just outside the city two attractions pull in visitors. **Heritage Park**, Blackrock, offers cameos of Cork life and the history of the Cork fire brigade, the only such fire service museum in Ire-land. Meanwhile, you can glimpse the fully restored 19th/early 20th century style cells of the **Cork City Gaol**. Oddly, the gaol now houses the national broadcasting museum.

County Cork

Cork is a good centre for excursions. **Blarney Castle** (open Mon–Sat: May 9am–6.30pm, Jun–Aug 9am–7pm, Sept 9am–6.30pm, Oct–Apr 9am–sunset – or 6pm; Sun: summer 9.30am–5.30pm, winter 9.30am–sunset) is 8km (5 miles) to the north. The original owner of the castle, Cormac Mac-Carthy, had a habit of employing soothing but evasive chatter (dubbed the 'blarney') as delaying tactics. Today, in order to acquire similar eloquence, tourists climb up to the battlement, lie flat on their backs, hang on to two iron bars and extend the head backwards in order to kiss an awkwardly placed stone. Most visitors play along with this preposterous legend.

The castle itself is worth a visit, even if mighty hordes of tourists do besiege it every summer. The formidable keep was built in the middle of the 15th century, while the private park, in which the castle stands, includes a cool, slightly mysterious dell with ancient occult connections.

In ports around the world, ships are seen with *Cobh* on the stern. **Cobh**, the south coast's largest seaport, lies about 24km (15 miles) east of Cork City. It is pronounced 'Cove', which is exactly what it means in Irish.

From Queen Victoria's visit in 1849, until 1922, Cobh was called Queenstown. The port is touched by nostalgia – from the days of the great transatlantic liners and the earlier, more tragic traffic of desperate emigrants fleeing the Irish famine

Cobh's majestic Cathedral of St Colman

for Canada or America. **The Queenstown Story** provides a particular insight into this era. The Cunard shipping office is now a bank. High above the harbour, the spire of the **Cathedral of St Colman** reaches heavenward. Recitals are given in the summer on the cathedral's 47-bell carillon.

In Midleton, to the northeast of Cobh, visit the **Old Midleton Distillery** (guided tours Mar–Oct: daily 10am– 6pm, last tour at 4.30pm; Nov–Feb: Mon–Fri at 11.30am, 2.30pm and 4pm) in a converted whiskey distillery that dates back to the late 18th century. It tells the story of Irish whiskey via an audiovisual presentation, and offers a tour with tastings.

The town of **Youghal** (in English pronounced 'Yawl'), east of Midleton, is a resort with 8km (5 miles) of beach and a long seafaring history. It is renowned for its fine lace, *point d'Irlande*. The town walls from the Middle Ages can still be seen.

On the site of the main town gate is the **clock tower** from 1776. The high street runs right through it with the structure's four narrow floors and belfry rising above an arched platform over the street. The attractive tower was once a prison, and insurrectionists were hanged from the windows to set an example to the populace.

The most impressive monument in Youghal, **St. Mary's Collegiate Church** (Church of Ireland), is thought to have been founded in the 5th century. Most of the present structure went up in the 13th century, with detailed restoration in the 19th. Among the monuments and tombs in the church is one built, in his own honour, by Richard Boyle, a wheeler-dealer of the Elizabethan age and the first Earl of Cork. Myrtle Grove, a superb 16th-century house near the churchyard entrance, was the home of Sir Walter Raleigh, once the mayor of Youghal. The heritage museum on the quayside gives an excellent account of the town's history.

Steep green hills shelter the seaport of **Kinsale**, about 29km (18 miles) south of Cork. As its big harbour is virtually landlocked, it is a joy to sailors and sightseers alike. For a community of fewer than 2,000 people, Kinsale is renowned for its restaurants, among the best in southwest Ireland.

Today, the picturesque **harbour** is used by fishing boats, sailing dinghies and yachts. Ashore, there are fortifications to explore, including the classic star-shaped **Charles Fort** (open daily 10am–6pm), the Norman church of St Multose, a museum containing the first town charter of Edward III, and the **Desmond Castle and Wine Museum**.

Migratory birds inhabit the **Old Head** of Kinsale, 16km (10 miles) beyond the town. A modern lighthouse here is the successor to a beacon dating back to pre-Christian times. It was off the Old Head that a German submarine torpedoed the world-famous liner, the *Lusitania,* on 7 May 1915, resulting in the loss of 1,500 lives. The inquest into the disaster was held in the Kinsale Court House.

The twisting valley from Kinsale to Cork

En route from Kinsale to Bantry, Clonakilty's **West Cork Model Railway Village** (open Jul–Aug: daily 10am–6pm; Feb, Jun Sept–Oct 11am–5pm) depicts the area's six towns, complete with a working model of the defunct West Cork Railway.

Kinsale was under siege of 1601 as Spanish troops, who'd sailed to aid the Irish against Queen Elizabeth, were defeated, sparking the 'flight of the Earls' (the exodus of the Irish nobility) and the redistribution of their lands.

In West Cork, the town of **Bantry** nestles between steep green hills and a tranquil bay. The main sight in Bantry itself is Bantry House, a part-Georgian, part-Victorian stately home set in tropical gardens. The tapestries, paintings and furnishing can be viewed on weekdays year round.

Heading counter-clockwise around the bay from Bantry, the highway weaves through more rocky hills until it descends upon **Glengarriff**, where the beauty of the setting and the pleasant climate account for its year-round popularity.

Ferries take you round the bay from Glengarriff to **Garinish Island**, a 15-hectare (37-acre) park run by the Office of Public Works. The flora comes from five continents, and the centrepiece of all the horticultural achievement is a stunning walled **Italian garden**, surrounding a pool, with the gentle air of a paradisiacal perfume factory. In the 19th century Garinish was a bleak military outpost. From the top of the Martello tower, sentries once kept a lookout for Napoleonic invasion fleets; today, you can survey the luxuriant hills around the bay.

County Kerry

By any standard this is a spectacular part of the world: the Atlantic in all its moods, lakes designed for lovers or poets, and steep, evergreen mountains. **Killarney**, the centre of the lakes district, is a good base from which to explore the area and

The Old Weir Bridge Rapids in Killarney

offers a variety of services from shelter and food to fishing tackle. Seeing the sights here can be accomplished in many ways – by car, coach, bicycle, boat or even by 'jaunting car' – a horse-drawn rig driven by a *jarvey* (guide) who knows the territory and how to tell a story.

Due to the difficult terrain and logistical problems, it is best to visit the **Gap of Dunloe** and **Lakes of Killarney** on a fully organised excursion, usually an all-day trip. The Gap, a wild gorge 6km (4 miles) long, can be traversed on a pony, in a pony trap or on foot. Sound effects underline the weirdness of the eerie rock-strewn scenery as echoes bounce off the mountains – **MacGillycuddy's Reeks** in the west (the highest range in Ireland), and to the east, **Purple Mountain**. The long trek leads to the shore of the Upper Lake, where the tour continues by boat. The scenery around the lakes – thick forests, stark crags and enchanted islands – could not be more romantic, but there's adventure, too: the **rapids** at Old Weir Bridge.

Muckross Abbey is a friary dating from the 15th century with a massive square tower, a cloister with Gothic arches on two sides, Norman or Romanesque on the others and an old, weathered yew tree. **Muckross House** (open daily 9am–5.30pm, 9.30am-6pm Jul and Aug), now a museum of Kerry crafts and folklore, is surrounded by outstanding gardens. It is also a traditional farm, with old-style buildings and varied animals, including Kerry cows, native to the county.

The 14th-century ruins of **Ross Castle** are set near old copper mines on a peninsula of Lower Lake. The castle's garrison surrendered to Cromwell in 1652, awed by the superstition that strange ships meant doom. Cromwell knew the legend and brought armed vessels from Kinsale.

Ring of Kerry

The **Ring of Kerry** may well be the most sensational 180km (112 miles) you have ever driven. The ring is a circular route through hills as steep and round as volcanoes on the way to a coast of rugged cliffs and the most enthralling seascapes. This round-trip can be made in either direction, but here we proceed clockwise. Set aside a whole day.

Leaving Killarney, the road goes past lush lakeland. The first town on the route, **Kenmare**, is famous for lacemaking and the fish which fill its estuary. North of the small resort of Castlecove, 3km (2 miles) off the main road, are the ruins of **Staigue Fort**. A 2,500-year-old stronghold and one of Ireland's main archaeological wonders, this almost circular structure measures about 27m (90ft) across with a 6m (18ft) wall.

Near Caherdaniel, **Derrynane House**, the home of Daniel O'Connell *(see page 18)*, has been fully restored and is now a museum (open Apr and Oct: Tues–Sun 1–5pm; May–Sept: Mon–Sat 9am–6pm and Sun 11am–7pm; Nov-Mar: Sat–Sun 1–5pm). Game fishing is one of the lures for visitors to Waterville, as well as the scenery nearby: pitiless granite mountains on one side of the road, green fields and the sea on the other.

A bridge connects **Valentia Island**, with its high cliffs and vegetation, to the mainland at Portmagee. The island was the European terminus of the first Atlantic cable (1866), making possible the first telegraphic contact with America.

Off Valentia, the Skelligs Rocks rise abruptly from the ocean, shrouded with mystery and birds. Take a trip to the Skelligs Heritage Centre or tour the islands in a boat.

On the north shore of the peninsula, hills plunge to sea-level and cliffs complete the descent. **Dingle Bay** seems startlingly wide and the Dingle Peninsula looks like another country.

From Glenbeigh to Killorglin, the head of the bay is almost totally protected from the rough sea by huge sandbars extending from either shore. **Rossbeigh Strand**, with its 6km (4 miles) of golden sand, is a dream beach.

The last town on the ring, **Killorglin**, saves all its energy for three days in August and a mad pagan pageant called the Puck Fair, during which time a mountain goat presides over round-the-clock festivities. To the north, **Tralee**, the administrative centre of County Kerry, owes its fame to the songwriter William Mulchinock (1820–64). *The Rose of Tralee* and its author are honoured in a monument in the town park. The rose

> To the east of Tralee, the town of Castleisland is the location of the Crag Cave (open daily mid-Mar to 1 Nov). Nearly nearly 4km (2½ miles) long and bristling with stalagmites and stalactites, this is one of the best show caves in Ireland.

also calls the tune of Tralee's annual festival in late August, when girls of Irish descent from many countries compete in a beauty contest, and the winner is crowned Rose of Tralee.

Kerry the Kingdom in Tralee offers three experiences all in one. Kerry in Colour is an audiovisual presentation of the splendours of Kerry; the County Museum details Kerry's history since 5000BC; and the Geraldine Experience reconstructs life in medieval Tralee. A steam railway, with a locomotive from the old Tralee-Dingle railway, links the town with the restored, 19th-century **windmill** at Blennerville, 3km (2 miles) away. Apart from these popular attractions,

Tralee is the principal gateway to the Dingle peninsula, a long, dramatic finger which points some 48km (30 miles) into the Atlantic Ocean. On the south shore, amidst rocky coves, a sandbar grows into an arc of beach jutting more than halfway across the bay. **Inch Strand's** 6km (4 miles) of sand slide gently into the sea. Behind the bathers, archaeologists putter about the dunes, where inhabitants of prehistoric ages left meaningful clues about their way of life.

The small fishing port and resort of **Dingle** claims to be the most westerly town in Europe. From here to land's end all the hamlets are Irish-speaking parts of the Gaeltacht *(see page 74)*, where folklore and traditional language are still preserved. This is very harsh farming country, where old stone walls are overrun with shrubs and hardy vines divide skimpy parcels of land into fields. You'll see the sheep grazing on even the most precipitous of hills.

Dingle's Inch Strand has miles of sandy beach backed by dunes

The western part of the peninsula is very rich territory for archaeologists. In one area, the Fahan group alone consists of an astonishing 400 *clocháns* (beehive-shaped stone huts), along with forts and other ancient structures. For a spectacular panorama, drive up the **Connor Pass** (at an altitude of 460m/1,500ft) and see the sea out to the north and south, and mountains and lakes on the east and west sides. In this part of the world you're isolated from everything but the wild fuschia and heather beside the road.

THE WEST

Limerick

By the time the waters of the River Shannon have reached Limerick in the west, they have flowed over 274km (170 miles) through thick and thin, from narrow streams and howling rapids to lakes and lochs. After Limerick, an important seaport and industrial centre, they still have another 97km (60 miles) to travel through the estuary to the open Atlantic.

Limerick's position at the meeting of the river and its tidal waters assured the city a long and often violent history. The Danes were first on the scene. Their belligerence provoked repeated attacks by the native Irish, who finally drove them out.

The Anglo-Normans in turn captured *Luimneach* – in English 'Bare Spot'. King John visited in 1210 and ordered the construction of a **bridge** and **castle** (open Apr–Oct: daily 10am–5.30pm; Nov–Mar 10.30am–4.30pm), which still survive and have been extensively renovated. However, most of the walls, behind which the townsfolk gathered during times of siege, were pulled down in the 18th century as the city grew.

The city endured its most memorable seige after the Battle of the Boyne (1690), when Irish supporters of James II *(see page 17)* retired to Limerick pursued by William of Orange. The losers lost again, but the Treaty of Limerick allowed them to leave with honour and guaranteed the Irish freedom of religion. This was repudiated by the English Parliament, so today Limerick carries the title of 'City of the Violated Treaty'.

The 800-year-old **St Mary's Cathedral** spans many eras of architecture and art. The great square tower complements the arched Irish-Romanesque west door, while 15th-century carved misericords under the choir seats show free-ranging imagination with representations of angels, animals and other figures in relief. The cathedral grounds form the background for a colourful historical audiovisual show.

St John's Cathedral was constructed in Neo-Gothic style and claims the highest spire in Ireland (85m/280ft). Next to the cathedral St John's Square is an elegant 18th-century urban ensemble. The waterfront Custom House contains the priceless Hunt collection of antiquities and *objets d'art*, currently kept by the University of Limerick. The 'limerick' poem comes from the merry refrain 'Will you come up to Limerick?', part of an old parlour game, in which participants had to make up a nonsense verse.

King John's Castle guards the Shannon's banks

Shannon Airport reinforces Limerick's historic role as a centre of commerce. It opened in 1945, making its mark before fast and nonstop transatlantic travel

Limerick's St Mary's Cathedral

became the order of the day. Waiting passengers were offered a diversion – the chance to buy luxury goods exempt from tax. Thus the world's first duty-free shop grew into a shopping centre.

Bunratty Castle (open Jun-Aug: daily 9am–6pm; Sept-May: 9.30am–5.30pm) is a busy tourist attraction about 5km (3 miles) from the airport. At night professional Irish entertainers in period costumes recreate medieval banquets for visitors.

A favourite attraction of the Bunratty tourist complex is the **Folk Park** (same hours as the castle) containing replicas of typical old houses of the Shannon region. The peat fires are kept burning, as if the people had just stepped out to milk a cow or catch a fish.

At the marina in **Kilrush**, the heritage centre details the history of the town and Scattery, a nearby island and Christian settlement. At Foynes, you can visit the flying boat museum, which has old newsreels among its many attractions.

Ennis has a 13th-century friary, which in the Middle Ages had 350 friars and 600 students. The buildings were expanded and revamped over the years, and fully renovated in the 1950s.

The Burren

Northwest of Ennis, around 520 sq km (200 sq miles) of County Clare belongs to **the Burren**. Glaciers and ages of erosion have created lime-stone pavements – horizon-tal slabs divided by fissures, like the aftermath of an earthquake. Though some-times described as a moon-scape, the Burren is anything but barren; it is a quiet world of small animals, birds, but-terflies and Mediterranean flowers. It may seem hostile

A frustrated general serving Oliver Cromwell famously condemned the desolate Burren as having 'not enough wood to hang a man, not enough water to drown him, not enough clay to cover his corpse'. Some visitors describe the area as a moonscape.

to human habitation, but the profusion of forts and tombs proves it supported a population for several centuries.

Geologists, botanists and archaeologists have field trips on the pavements, and speleologists enjoy the caves. More than 40km (25 miles) of caves have been fully explored. Most are for experts only, but anyone can visit **Aillwee Cave**, southeast of Ballyvaughan (open April to October). In Kilfenora, a village on the edge of this plain, citizens have established the **Display Centre** as a quick and pleas-ant way to get your bearings. Kilfenora Cathedral, dating from the 12th century, is noted for its sculptured mon-uments and high crosses.

The **Cliffs of Moher**, 10km (6 miles) northwest of ◀ Lahinch, tower 215m (700ft) over the Atlantic Ocean. From **O'Brien's Tower** (open Mar–Oct: daily 9.30am– 5pm), an outpost near to the edge, the cliff-faces stand above the sea in horizontal layers as easily defined as the storeys of a glass skyscraper. Great waves crash against the foot of the cliff but the thump is heard late, like the report of a distant artillery shell. The cliffs are populated by thousands of seabirds .

The town of **Lisdoonvarna** is famous as a spa and has an atmosphere of romance. The springs produce waters rich in minerals, including sulphur, iron and iodine – thought to be good for rheumatic conditions and as a general tonic.

Across the border in County Galway, the area around Gort has a number of historic (not to mention powerful) literary associations. Lady Gregory, cofounder of the Abbey Theatre, lived in **Coole Park** (open daily 10am–5pm, 10am–6pm July–Aug), now a national forest with a heritage centre. The novel 'autograph tree' is inscribed with the initials of some of her famous visitors – Augustus John, John Masefield, Sean O'Casey and one of the very few who is instantly recognized by his initials: George Bernard Shaw.

Northeast of Gort, W.B. Yeats bought himself a 16th-century tower, **Thoor Ballylee** (open May–Sept: daily 10am– 6pm). He would wander around this piece of romantic architecture, an ideal place for inspiration with its spiral stairwell, alcoves and just outside the window, its very own burbling stream.

O'Brien's Tower offers great views of the Atlantic

Galway

The main city of the western province of Connacht, **Galway** is a port, resort, administrative and cultural centre. In medieval times it prospered as a city-state, but withered in the 17th century after prolonged sieges by the forces of Thomas Cromwell and, four

> Though not very romantic in itself, Lisdoonvarna has gained a reputation as a matchmaking mecca. People from all over the country arrive in Lisdoonvarna in an attempt to find a mate, making Ireland's first spa their last resort.

decades later, by William of Orange. Remnants of the old glory still shine in a few corners of the renewed city.

The **Collegiate Church of St Nicholas** was begun by the Anglo-Normans in 1320. Following local tradition, Columbus came to pray here before his voyage to America. The locals like to think he was checking out the 6th-century transatlantic explorer, St Brendan. The pyramid-shaped steeple on top of the triple-naved church is full of stone carvings.

During Galway's heyday 14 families, mostly of Welsh and Norman descent, formed a sort of medieval Mafia that controlled the economic and political life of the town. Their common enemy, the O'Flaherty family, inspired the inscription (1549) over the old town gate: 'From the fury of the O'Flaherties, good Lord deliver us'.

Of the tribes in Galway, the Lynch family left the most memories and monuments. **Lynch's Castle**, a town house dating from 1600, is decorated with excellent stonework, gargoyles and carved window frames. This rare building has been restored and houses a bank.

Another reminder of the Lynches is the Lynch Memorial Window, with a plaque recounting the macabre story of James Lynch Fitzstephen – Mayor of Galway in 1493 – who condemned and executed his own son, Walter, for murder. Judge Lynch had to be the hangman because nobody else would agree to carry out the sentence.

Galway's Catholic cathedral – whose full name is **Cathedral of Our Lady Assumed into Heaven and St Nicholas** – has a giant dome looming over the city. The classical architecture is misleading; the church was dedicated in 1965. Alongside the cathedral is Galway's **Salmon Weir**, in which salmon fight their way from the sea up to the lakeland. From June to July you can see them queueing up for a chance to leap up the falls and follow their instincts to sweet water.

Galway's beauty is reflected in its rivers, canals and bays

In Galway you can also visit the restored house of **Bowling Green**, the one-up, one-down dwelling where James Joyce's wife, Nora Barnacle, was brought up. It is now home to the **Nora Barnacle House Museum** (open May–Sept: Mon–Sat 10am–7pm). Letters, photographs and other memorbilia from the lives of the couple make a visit here a unique experience.

Galway's seaside suburb, **Salthill**, is a hugely popular resort with rocky seawalls and beaches of fine sand. It's a great place to watch the sun set on Galway Bay; sprawling hills enclose most of the bay, but the Atlantic can be seen to the west.

Connemara

Lough Corrib, a loch extending 43km (27 miles) north from Galway, is big enough to be whipped by waves when the wind hurtles down the hillside. It's generally shallow and well supplied with islands and fish – salmon, trout, pike and perch. Lough Corrib divides County Galway into two contrasting regions: a fertile limestone plain to the east, and Connemara – a range of dramatic mountains and sparkling lakes – to the west, all enclosed by the coastline of rugged cliffs and pristine beaches.

The huge Twelve Bens of Connemara ('ben' is Gaelic for peak) constitute a range of moody mountains mostly inhabited by sheep; the foothills are interspersed with bogs and pretty lakes.

Much of Connemara is an Irish-speaking enclave. This is also the home of the Connemara pony – robust, intelligent and self-reliant. Spanish horses of the 16th century are rumoured to have crossbred with Irish ponies; one version says that the stallions swam ashore from ships of the Spanish Armada wrecked on nearby rocks.

The sky seems to change by the minute in the far west – dazzling sun, fleeting clouds and rain alternating so quickly that photographers have to be constantly at the ready. The capital is the well-placed market town of **Clifden**, a base for exploring the nearby lakes and rivers, as well as fine beaches, bogs and mountains. The town's Irish name is *An Clochan*, meaning 'Stepping Stones'. There are so many areas of water around Clifden that you can't tell the genuine sea inlets from the coves of the lakes, except for the seaweed, a plant which features in Irish cooking more than you'd expect. Nearby is **Kylemore Abbey**, the home of Ireland's Benedictine nuns and one of the most photographed buildings in the country (open daily).

The idyllically located Kylemore Abbey

Killary Harbour, near Leenane, offers superb anchorage protected by mountains on both sides. The floats and rafts are busy farming mussels. Funnily enough, the Irish don't think all that much of seafood, so a lot of it is exported to France where there are more seafood enthusiasts.

Aran Islands

Out in the Atlantic, 48km (30 miles) off Galway, the **Aran Islands** are a remote outpost indeed, little more than stone outcrops. In the past islanders had to struggle to survive, cultivating the bleak limestone terrain, which had so little topsoil that they would ship it in from the mainland or scrape it from the cracks between the rocks and mix it with seaweed fertiliser to grow feed for their livestock. Tourism has now improved their fortunes, and though their famous Aran sweaters are still made here, these days few of them are hand-knitted. All the locals speak Gaelic, but most speak English too.

Inishmore, 'the Big Island' as the Aran folk call it, is 14km (9 miles) from tip to tip and only 3km (2 miles) across. From the air – and you can fly there from Galway – you can make out tapestries of tiny fields enclosed by dry-stone walls. Inishmore's one and only real village, **Kilronan**, has a port where ferries from the mainland dock. The fishermen work aboard modern trawlers, but the traditional *currachs,* tar-coated boats with canvas hulls, are still used. Kilronan's heritage centre gives a good insight into island life. This is an island to explore on foot or rented bicycle. If you're in a hurry, you can hire pony traps for guided tours, or the island even has a single motorised taxi which doubles as a school bus.

The remarkable monument of **Dún Aengus** (open Mar–Oct: daily 10am–6pm; Nov–Feb: 11.30am–3.30pm), a giant prehistoric fortress on the sheer edge of a cliff some 91m (300ft) high, is about a 15-minute walk across the fields from the road. Three layers of stone walls, the outermost 6m (20ft) high, surround the courtyard 46m (150ft) across. With the ramparts and obstacles set up beyond the wall, the total area covers 4 hectares (11 acres). Even in modern times it would take a rash general to stage an attack on Dún Aengus.

Elsewhere on the islands, among colourful wild flowers, grazing cows, sheep and an abundance of bounding rabbits, there are numerous **archaeological sites** of less importance, that nevertheless have their own diversion to offer. Here you'll find stone forts and groups of primitive stone dwellings, as well as hermits' cells, round towers and ruined churches.

Dún Aengus

Farming is big business

In striking contrast to these traditional structures, a large, glass-walled factory sits in the west of Inishmore. The time-honoured dexterity of the Aran women has been fully diverted from the local, hardy wool to modern technology; they now spend their time manufacturing electronic components.

County Mayo

Rising high above Clew Bay, **Croagh Patrick** is Ireland's Holy Mountain. Compared to Ireland's other mountains, this holy peak looks more like a black slag heap. Even so, each year thousands of pilgrims ascend the imposing summit. St Patrick is said to have spent Lent here in 441. There are views of the bay and the hills of counties Mayo, Clare and Galway.

Westport, at the head of Clew Bay, is an example of 18th-century urban planning. The Mall boulevard follows the Carrowbeg River. Outside the town, the home of the Marquess of Sligo can be visited. **Westport House** (open Easter weekend & Sundays during May: 2–5pm; Jun: daily 2–5pm; Jul–Aug: daily 11.30am–5.30pm; Sept: daily 2–5pm) is palatial, with paintings, silver and glassware. There's a souvenir shop, go-cart rides for children and even a dungeon.

Inland, the village of **Knock** (from the Irish *Cnoc Mhuire* – 'Mary's Hill') is a respected place of pilgrimage. In 1879 the townspeople saw an apparition of the Virgin Mary, St Joseph and St John on a south gable of the old parish church. In the centenary year of 1979, pilgrim Pope John Paul II came from Rome to address an open-air mass at Knock with over 400,000 of the faithful. Getting here is easy, thanks to the small international airport, and Knock still caters to the pilgrims, with souvenir shops and a museum of folklore and handicrafts. The site of the famous apparition has been enclosed in glass, and statues recreate the position of the figures in the vision.

Cruising The River Shannon

The best place to hire a boat is Carrick-on-Shannon, the capital of County Leitrim and home to the superb Costello Chapel. Downstream, the river runs into Lough Corry, the first of many interconnected lakes in the Shannon basin. **Lough Ree**, halfway down, is 26km (16 miles) long and 11km (7 miles) wide, with deserted wooded islands.

The main cross-country roads ford the Shannon at the central market town of **Athlone**, with a medieval castle overlooking the Shannon Bridge. The town holds a number of festivals and cultural events (www.athelonechamber.ie). At a bend in the river is **Clonmacnoise**, an ancient monastic settlement founded in the 6th century by St Ciaran. Nearby you can follow a 9-km (5½-mile) trip along the Clonmacnoise & West Offaly Railway.

Just 6km (4 miles) south of Clonmacnoise, a 16-arch bridge marks Shannonbridge; at Shannon Harbour the Grand Canal from Dublin meets the river. Portumna is a fishing and boating resort with a new marina.

Lough Derg is the largest of the Shannon lakes – 40km (25 miles) long and up to 5km (3 miles) wide with islets and fair green hills beyond – a perfect end to the trip. This is just as well because dangerous rapids abound below **Killaloe**, a prudent place to abandon ship. Killaloe was once a great ecclesiastical centre, where **St Flannan's Cathedral** has been restored to its 12th-century glory. The richly carved Romanesque doorway is said to be the entrance to the tomb of King Murtagh O'Brien of Munster (d. 1120). The granite shaft nearby, from about the year 1,000, bears a bilingual inscription in Runic and Ogham letters – a foretaste of today's Irish-English road signs.

In the town of **Foxford**, an interpretative centre tells the story of the old woollen mills and the famine in the area, while near Ballycastle, on the north Mayo cliffs, the pyramid-shaped heritage centre of **Céide Fields** (open daily 10am–5pm; to 6pm in summer) reveals the ancient history of the many prehistoric settlements in the area. The site is estimated to be the single largest Stone Age monument in existence in the world today. It dates as far back as 3000BC.

➤ The country's biggest island, **Achill**, is buffeted by wind and tide, with meagre farms between ominous mountains and rocky shores. Despite this (or because of it) the scenery – from enormous cliffs to superb beaches – is truly magnificent. Achill feels adrift, though you can drive there from the mainland across an unimpressive bridge. Driving on the island's deserted roads can revive the joy of motoring.

Near Keel, **Trawmore Strand** is an outstanding model of a long, white-sand beach. Keel's large nine-hole golf course spreads to the dunes and suffers no shortage of bunkers.

Prehistoric graves can be found on the harsh slopes of Achill's overpoweringly high mountain, the 672-m (2,204-ft) **Slievemore**. Driving offers the most vertigo-inducing cliff views and perspectives of the ocean churning round the off-islands and shoals. Inland, note the three-chimneyed cottages set between moors and bogs.

Shamrock Curtain

Travelling in the west of Ireland you may cross the Shamrock Curtain, an important cultural frontier. Signs are printed in Gaelic letters and the people speak Irish as a first language. This is the Gaeltacht. It makes up the main line of resistance to the English language. The Dublin government actively supports Gaeltacht efforts to keep the old language and culture alive. Courses in Irish are offered here every summer.

THE NORTHWEST

Sligo lies between two mountains, Ben Bulben and Knocknarea. Early fame came to the town in 807 when the Vikings invaded. In 1252 Maurice Fitzgerald, the Earl of Kildare, founded **Sligo Abbey** (open Apr–Oct: daily 10am–6pm), a Dominican friary. It burned down in 1414, but was rebuilt soon afterwards. Then it was attacked by Puritan troops in 1641, and the friars were killed. Its ruins combine desolation and grace. Three sides have been preserved, and there are fine carvings.

The resort of **Strandhill**, west of Sligo, has a beach with long-rolling waves for surfers. **Knocknarea**, the flat-topped mountain over this stretch of shore, must have had a strange attraction for the early settlers, as the area has an abundance of megalithic monuments. On the 329-m (1,078-ft) summit of Knocknarea there is a cairn (tomb of stones). Legend says it is the burial place of the 1st-century Queen Maeve of Connaught. Facing Strandhill, on the opposite side of the harbour, are the resorts of Rosses Point and Coney Island, after which, it is said, New York's amusement park was named.

W.B. Yeats, who spent many childhood summer holidays here, is buried near the front door of the town's

W.B. Yeats statue, Sligo

small church, with its turreted belfry in the shadow of the awesome **Ben Bulben**, 527m (1,730ft) high. On its flat top you'll find arctic and alpine plants.

About 27km (17 miles) to the north of Sligo, situated on the approach to the village of Mullaghmore, look out for the stunning **Classiebawn Castle**, which claims the skyline all to itself. This was the summer dwelling of Earl Mountbatten of Burma, who was assassinated by the IRA in 1979 when his fishing boat was blown up just off the shore nearby.

County Donegal

The most northerly county on the island, Donegal is known for its scenery – mountains, glens and lakes. This is also where Donegal homespun **tweed** comes from. Donegal's medieval **castle** occupies the site of a previous Viking fort. (*Dun na nGall* in Irish means the 'Fortress of the Foreigners', a refer-

Donegal's rolling landscape is ideal for crops

ence to the Vikings.) On the edge of town, the ruins of Donegal Abbey overlook the estuary. West along the coast, **Killybegs** is a big fishing port; the trawlers here have wheelhouses with devices for tracking down the fish.

The road to the village of **Glencolumbkille** heads deep into spectacular country. Over the crest of a hill, you see the simple village below, enfolded in green hillsides

Donegal's Green Gate is one of Ireland's best B&Bs

that funnel down to the sea. In Irish the name *Glencolumbkille* means the 'Glen of St Colmcille' (or St Columba).

Today it is said that the 6th-century saint, who changed the course of history by introducing the Christian faith to Scotland, began his career by converting locals. The numerous old **standing stones** were formerly pagan monuments which St Columba simply adapted to the new religion. On the saint's feast day, 9 June, pilgrims follow the pathway of these old stones. Over 40 prehistoric *dolmens*, *souterrains* and cairns have been catalogued in this area, some as old as 5,000 years.

Between Derry and Letterkenny, you can visit the **stone fort** built in prehistoric times, which is well-preserved and similar in style to Staigue Fort in County Kerry. **Fort Dunree**, on the Inishowen peninsula overlooking Lough Swilly, is a fascinating military history museum in an old fort.

Glenveagh National Park forms 10,000 hectares (24,700 acres) of the most beautiful part of Co. Donegal, including Glenveagh Castle and Glebe House, built in 1828 in graceful Regency style and sumptuously furnished. It was once the home of Derek Hill, the artist, who gave it to the Irish nation.

NORTHERN IRELAND

Surprisingly for such an historically troubled area, it's some-times hard to be sure of the exact location of the border between the Republic and Northern Ireland. Partly this is because it snakes its way along 18th-century county bound-aries through farming land that is sometimes bleak, more often breathtakingly beautiful, taking little account of natural bound-aries such as rivers, or of the cultural differences that separate Republican-minded Roman Catholics and British-oriented Protestants. Houses straddle it so that, as the joke has it, a man may sleep with his head in the United Kingdom and his heart in the Republic of Ireland.

Political expediency accounts for the absurdities. It had been intended to redraw the border rationally after partition in 1920 left six of the nine counties of the ancient province of Ulster

Glenelly Valley, in the Sperrins

(Antrim, Down, Armagh, Derry, Fermanagh and Tyrone) under British rule, and a Boundary Commission was set up to advise. But in the end the British and Irish governments, both hoping to avoid further trouble, suppressed the commission's report and left things as they were. Had they decided differently, much of the subsequent conflict might have been averted.

Belfast City Hall

Belfast

Belfast (pop. 400,000) looks little different from a provincial English city. Donegall Place, its 'main street', is lined with UK multiple stores such as Marks & Spencer, Next and Boots; while mailboxes and telephone kiosks look exactly the same as they do in Birmingham or Liverpool. In the city centre at least, there's little evidence of sectarian tension. Indeed, the Troubles are being mined for profit, as bus and taxi tours offer to show visitors where the worst riots of the 1970s and '80s took place.

Set in a saucer of green hills and spanning the mouth of the River Lagan as it flows into the Irish Sea, Belfast is essentially a Victorian creation, its wealth founded on textile manufacturing and shipbuilding. It was Ireland's only industrial city but today most of the factories have vanished, though two towering yellow cranes (Samson and Goliath) survive as a reminder of the great days of Harland & Wolff shipyard, builder of the *Titanic*. Depression has been confined mainly to economics and politics, however, for Belfast people have a sharp wit and a restless energy that make the city a lively place.

Dominating the centre in Donegall Square is the 1906 **City Hall** (guided tours available; free), whose architecture has been dubbed 'Wrenaissance' in tribute to its shameless resemblance to St Paul's Cathedral in London. Queen Victoria presides outside, her statue supported by toilers from the linen and shipbuilding industries. Inside, an ornate marble staircase sweeps up to the Rotunda, and the banqueting hall and council chamber are suitably grandiloquent. Among the marble statues around the City Hall is a **Titanic Memorial**, complete with weeping sea-nymphs.

To the north of the City Hall, Donegall Place, which becomes Royal Avenue, is Belfast's main shopping thoroughfare. **Linen Hall Library**, on Donegall Square North, is a revered public-subscription library – a treasure house for historians and political journalists. A couple of hundred yards to the west, on College Square East, is the city's finest building,

The Crown Liquor Saloon: Belfast's most intoxicating of landmarks

the red-brick **Royal Belfast Academical Institution**, designed by Sir John Soane in 1807. Close by, on Great Victoria Street, are two architectural gems: the 1895 **Grand Opera House**, with its plush brass and velvet, its gilded elephant heads and its excellent acoustics, and the **Crown Liquor Saloon**, a riot of Victorian Baroque owned by the National Trust

Queen's University

but still serving the finest Guinness and whiskies.

The restaurant-rich Great Victoria Street leads on, via Shaftesbury Square, to the Tudor-style **Queen's University**, whose central tower bears a suspicious resemblance to that of Magdalen College, Oxford. The university has colonised just about every available building in the vicinity, but welcome green space is provided by the adjacent **Royal Botanic Gardens**, which contain a curvilinear Palm House. Beside the park is the **Ulster Museum** (open Mon–Fri 10am–5pm, Sat 1–5pm, Sun 2–5pm), noted for well-presented displays of Irish art from the Bronze Age onwards. One attraction is the treasure trove rescued from the Spanish Armada ship *Gerona*, wrecked off the North Antrim coast in 1588.

Belfast, of course, has many churches. Worth checking out are the neo-Romanesque **St Anne's Cathedral** in Donegall Street, the extravagantly decorated interior of **St Malachy's Church** in Clarence Street and the delightful **First Presbyterian Church** in Rosemary Street.

On the Newtownards Road, 10km (6 miles) from the centre, is the much televised intended seat of government, **Parliament Buildings**, echoing the pomp of Buckingham Palace.

The Giant's Causeway, created when hot lava met cold sea

The Antrim Coast Road

To the northeast of Belfast, past **Carrickfergus** (which has a fine Norman castle) and the dull port of **Larne**, the lovely **Antrim Coast Road** runs alongside the Irish Sea through picturesque villages such as **Cushendall** and **Cushendun**. Diversions can be made along the way into any of the nine green glens, peaceful landscapes traditionally farmed.

The north coast begins at **Ballycastle**, setting for an end-of-August agricultural fair that has been held since 1606, and the ferry departure point for a 13-km (8-mile) trip to **Rathlin Island**, whose population of 100 is vastly outnumbered by seabirds. Continuing east, you pass **Carrick-a-Rede Rope Bridge**, which swings over a 24-m (80-ft) chasm, allowing salmon fishermen and brave tourists access to a rocky promontory. Past cliffs and white surfers' beaches are the romantic ruins of the 6th-century **Dunseverick Castle**.

Bushmills is home to the world's oldest distillery (tours and whiskey tastings available). It is also the jumping-off point for Ireland's most spectacular natural phenomenon, the **Giant's Causeway**. Formed 60 million years ago when molten lava froze into 38,000 basalt columns, mostly hexagonal, it looks like a series of giant stepping-stones. You can park near the Causeway or, in season, catch a narrow-gauge steam locomotive from Bushmills. To the west are the resorts of **Portrush** and **Portstewart**, as well as the ruins of the 14th-century **Dunluce Castle**.

Derry City and Fermanagh

Protestants still call Northern Ireland's second city Londonderry, the name given to it by the London guilds who began creating it in 1614 as the last walled city in Europe. The 6-m (20-ft) thick walls come complete with watchtowers and cannon such as the 1642 'Roaring Meg'. The excellent **Tower Museum**, in Union Hall Place, relates the city's troubled history. **St Columb's Cathedral**, in London Street, is a graceful 17th-century Anglican church built in Planters' Gothic style.

Music and Murals

Northern Ireland's popular culture portrays the sectarian divide with the bluntness of bombs and bullets. Triumphalist or threatening murals adorn the sides of hundreds of houses, particularly in Belfast and Derry. The Protestant versions often feature William of Orange, who defeated his Catholic father-in-law, James II, at the Battle of the Boyne in 1690. Catholic murals celebrate Republican heroes and aspirations. Balaclava-clad men brandishing rifles are common to both traditions. The worst murals are crudely executed; the best can be evaluated as folk art.

For both Protestants and Catholics, marching bands keep history alive and mark out territory. The biggest parades are staged on 12 July by Protestant Orangemen (commemorating William of Orange). On the surface it's tuneful pageantry – but it can also be fiercely provocative.

Boa Island's Janus statue

Near Omagh, 56km (35 miles) to the south, is the **Ulster-American Folk Park** (open Apr–Sept: Mon–Sat 10.30am–4.30pm, Sun 11am–5pm; Oct–Mar: Mon–Fri 10.30am–3.30pm). The rebuilt craftsmen's cottages, schoolhouse and forge recreate 18th-century living conditions here, while log cabins and covered wagons illustrate the New World the many emigrants created in America. It is claimed that 11 US presidents had their roots in the province.

Further south, **Fermanagh** is the province's lakeland playground. Summer pleasure boats ply the lakes from the busy county town of **Enniskillen**. On Lower Lough Erne, **Boa Island** has an ancient two-faced Janus statue, radiating Celtic inscrutability, and **Devenish Island** has a fine round tower.

Heading back towards the east coast, it's worth stopping at **Armagh**, which has two fine cathedrals (both called St Patrick's), some notable Georgian buildings and a planetarium. Just outside the town is **Navan Fort**, Europe's oldest Celtic site.

Mountains of Mourne

Close to the Irish Sea, the 15 granite peaks of the **Mourne Mountains** reach to more than 600m (2,000ft). At the summit of Slieve Donard are two cairns (ancient mounds of stones). From here, on a clear day, you can see Scotland, England, the Isle of Man and Snowdonia in Wales.

Passing through **Downpatrick**, a sedate market town, you can take the ferry from Strangford to Portaferry and drive up the **Ards Peninsula**, a 37-km (23-mile) finger dotted by villages and beaches. **Mount Stewart**, an 18th-century mansion, has one of Europe's greatest gardens, its microclimate nourishing a vast variety of plants, shrubs and trees.

At Cultra, near Holywood on the main road into Belfast, the **Ulster Folk and Transport Museum** (open Mar–Jun: Mon–Fri 10am–5pm, Sat 10am–6pm, Sun 11am–6pm; Jul–Sept: Mon–Sat 10am–6pm, Sun 11am–6pm; Oct–Feb: Mon–Sat 10am–4pm, Sun 11am–5pm) is set in 70 hectares (170 acres) of a green and picnic-friendly woodland park. Old farmhouses, mills and even a church were moved with painstaking labour, stone by stone, from their original sites all over Ulster to be preserved in one spot, forming an agricultural, industrial and social history. The large and impressive transport collection contains old carriages and bicycles, steam locomotives, cars and aircraft.

Mount Stewart house and gardens

WHAT TO DO

SPORTS

Whether on land or sea (or river or lake), the Irish enjoy so many sporting activities that we can only touch on a handful of the most popular. If you are interested in more esoteric sports, such as hang-gliding, orienteering, or even polo, the tourist board *(see page 122)* can put you in touch with the appropriate sports associations.

Sports Ashore

Golf: In a country so green, you might scarcely notice the vast number of golf courses, but there are more than 600, including several of championship status. Some clubs are private, but not rigorously so: while you might find that non-members are excluded over the weekend, you'll have few problems on weekdays. In between rounds you can always keep in shape with pitch and putt, a traditional Irish game somewhere between mini-golf and the real thing, played with a putter and one other club. See <www.golfingireland.com> for more details.

Greyhound racing: This is a very popular pursuit on the island. Teams of hare-brained dogs keep eager gamblers busy six nights a week in Dublin – which has two greyhound stadiums – and elsewhere in Ireland.

Horse racing: Almost everyone in Ireland seems to be totally engrossed, one way or another, in the sport of kings. Dublin boasts several famous courses within easy reach on a day-trip. The flat season is from March to November, and steeplechasing goes on all year. See <www.hri.ie> for information on events.

Sailing between the peninsulas of Dingle

Horse riding: Stables can be found all over Ireland with fine Irish horses, beautiful ponies, and trekking routes through delightful verdant countryside; <www.ehi.ie> lists establishments that specially cater for holiday makers.

Tennis: Many hotels advertise their own courts, some of them with instructors, but elsewhere there are public courts, including those in many Dublin parks.

National games: Hurling is a very fast variant of hockey, in which a small, leather-covered ball is struck with a hurley – similar to a hockey stick. Gaelic football, the other traditional Irish game, includes elements of both soccer and rugby. For more information on gaelic sporting events and history, go to <www.gaa.ie>.

With a large selection of stables, getting on a horse is no problem

Imported games: Football <www.fai.ie> and rugby <www.irishrugby.ie> leagues are very popular, and cricket is widely played.

Sports on the Water

Sailing: Any seasoned old salt with a seaworthy yacht will no doubt welcome the challenges of the west coast, but first-time sailors will be better off handling conditions off the south and east coasts and in the bays all around the island. Ask the tourist board *(see page 122)* for details about boat rental and sailing fees.

Sea fishing: From a long sandy beach, a pier, a clifftop or a boat, you can hook big beautiful trophies of the deep, such as shark, sea bass, tope, skate, halibut, conger and many more.

Swimming: The tourist board's information sheet *(see page 122)* on seaside resorts lists a dozen; the beaches come in all shapes and sizes, but have one thing in common: no crowds.

Surfing: The heavy Atlantic swells are more impressive on the west and north coasts, and so offer better surfing.

Boating: River cruising is very popular. You can also try more energetic sports such as canoeing on lakes or rivers.

Game fishing: Fertile salmon fisheries are mostly restricted, but arrangements can be made – though preferably well in advance. Trout are abundant in rivers and lakes; as with salmon, you will need a licence.

SHOPPING

Friendly sales staff help make shopping in Ireland a real pleasure. The appealing products here are made by Irish craftsmen in traditional or new styles.

Aran sweaters: These fishermen's sweaters can be easily recognised. Demand so far exceeds supply that they are now made in mainland factories as well as in the cottages on the Aran islands. Be sure to check your garment is genuinely handknitted.

Connemara marble: A rich green, this stone is made into all sorts of souvenirs.

Crafts: An array of enamel dishes, plaques and pendants by local craftsmen.

Crosses: Reproductions of old Christian crosses and St Brigid crosses made out of straw.

Dolls: Dressed in traditional regional costumes.

Glassware: Waterford crystal, world renowned, is once

Ireland's more sophisticated crafts make great souvenirs

again a busy concern. Crystal is also made in Kilkenny, Tipperary, Cavan, Dublin, Galway and Tyrone.

Jewellery: Celtic designs and illustrations from the ancient Book of Kells inspire today's goldsmiths and silversmiths.

Kinsale smocks: These hardy cotton wind-cheaters are made for local sailors – not to be confused with Kinsale cloaks, traditional dress now revived as chic evening-wear.

Lace: Although a waning trade in Limerick and County Monaghan, there is now a strong revival of lace-making in Carrickmacross, Clones, Kenmare and Youghal.

Linen: Weaving continues in Northern Ireland and is sold everywhere in the country.

Paintings: Irish-based artists produce fine studies of Ireland, including landscapes, seascapes, flora and fauna, in oils, watercolors and pen and wash. Works are widely available and well priced.

Peat: Even the turf of Ireland is compressed and sculpted to reproduce ancient religious and folklore symbols.

Pottery: Traditional and modern designs in kitchenware.

Rushwork: In a land rich in thatched cottages, the makers of woven baskets and similar wickerwork still thrive.

Smoked salmon: A souvenir you can eat that is specially packed for travelling, and on sale at the airport.

Souvenirs: Leprechauns in all sizes, worry stones made of marble, elegant Irish coffee glasses and *shillelaghs* (short wooden clubs) are all widely available. Books about every aspect of Irish life and its history make easy-to-carry souvenirs.

Tweed: Handwoven fabrics in a variety of colors and weights, ideal for overcoats, jackets or light shawls.

NIGHTLIFE

Many hotels and pubs present cabaret nights featuring the most diverse cross-section of traditional Irish entertainment possible: folk singers, harpists, dancers and storytellers. In local pubs the programme may consist of a lone folk singer with guitar. At the other end of the scale the luxury hotels put on elaborate productions.

The shows have a typically Irish mixture of hand-clapping high spirits and 'Come Back to Erin' nostalgia. Jigs and reels are tirelessly danced, and lively tap dancers revive some of the country's oldest and best routines. Harps

Temple Bar is one of Dublin's liveliest areas

and banjos, bagpipes and accordions are all played with gusto. Fast fiddlers are as ubiquitous here as gypsy violinists in Budapest, though they tend to be a lot more cheerful.

You will find less polished versions of traditional Irish music at *fleadhanna*, festivals of music and song around the island, climaxing in the all Ireland *Fleadh* in the summer (August). Tourist offices will have detailed schedules of such events.

Dublin has a lively **nightclub** scene, with music for all tastes. Lower Leeson Street, the leading nightspot, has become somewhat passé, with **Temple Bar** <www.temple-bar.ie> in the city centre becoming more appealing to younger crowds seeking entertainment. The more up-to-date nightclubs usually offer witty and fast-talking DJs or other artists, food, drink and very often a celebrity or two from the worlds of film and music.

Easy access to the outdoors makes Ireland a good venue for families

Restored medieval castles are used for another kind of night out – grandiose candlelit **banquets** with traditional stories, poems and songs. These recreations of lusty celebrations from the past are professionally arranged. If you have no car you can join package tours that include door-to-door transportation.

Ireland's grand **theatrical** tradition – which gave the world Goldsmith, Shaw, Sheridan, Beckett O'Casey and Behan – continues in some major towns such as Dublin, Belfast and Cork. The Abbey Theatre <www.abbeytheatre.ie>, Dublin, is still packing them in after more than 75 years. Newspapers usually print full listings of theatrical events as well as concerts and films.

CHILDREN IN IRELAND

Fun activities for children of all ages can be found throughout the country at:

● **Bray promenade**, 19km (12 miles) south of Dublin. A big seaside resort with dodgems and a seafront aquarium.

● **Clara-Lara**, Vale of Clara, County Wicklow, tel: (0404) 46161. Fun park, trout farm and amusements for children of all ages. Open summer only.

● **Dublin Zoo**, tel: (01) 677 1425. A wide variety of animals. Café and restaurant. <www.dublinzoo.ie>.

● **Farm visits**. In numerous regions farms are open to visitors and offer a warm welcome to children. Tourist information offices *(see page 122)* have full details.

● **Fota Wildlife Park and Arboretum,** near the town of Cobh, County Cork, tel: (021) 481 2678. Large wildlife park, open mid-March–October. <www.fotawildlife.ie>.

● **Irish National Heritage Park,** near Wexford, tel: (053) 20733. A collection of full-sized replicas of Irish buildings from prehistoric to Norman times. Open mid-March–October. <www.inhp.com>.

● **Kilmainham Gaol,** Dublin, tel: (01) 453 5984. The historic jail where leaders of the 1916 rising were executed, now a heritage centre. Open all year, every day.

● **National Gallery of Ireland**, Merrion Square West, Dublin 2. Irish work, Dutch masters, frequent children's activities. <www.nationalgallery.ie>.

● **National Wax Museum**, Franby Row, off Parnell Square, Dublin 1, tel: (01) 872 6340. Wax figures, chamber of horrors.

● **Newbridge Demesne**, County Dublin, tel: (01) 843 6534. An 18th-century house with farm and animals.

● **Straffan Steam Museum**, in County Kildare, tel: (01) 628 8412, has model and full-sized steam engines <www.steam-museum.ie>.

Eating on the hoof in Dublin

The **butterfly farm** in County Kildare, tel: (01) 627 1109, has a large number of butterflies as well as scary, hairy tarantulas and myriad other poisonous spiders. Open in May, June and July only.

Tralee, in Co. Kerry. Steam train runs from the town to Blennerville, a restored early 19th-century windmill only 3km (2 miles) away.

Westport House, Westport, County Mayo, tel: (098) 25430. There are play facilities for children, plus a zoo and a steam railway.

Calendar of Events

As dates frequently change, we advise you to contact the local tourist office for up-to-date information on particular festivals.

March: *St Patrick's Week* – celebrations in Dublin and other towns throughout the country; *Belfast Film Festival* – a chance to bring international cinema to Ireland and offer a platform for local film-makers who struggle to break into the mainstream.

April: *The Cork International Choral Festival*. The famous Irish Grand National horse race; *Dublin International Film Festival*.

May: *Cork International Choral and Folk Dance Festival; Dublin Spring Show and Industries Fair; Dundalk Maytime Festival* – classical music in great Irish houses (late May); *Killarney Pan-Celtic Week* – competitions and cultural events which enjoy the participation of other Celtic countries; *Listowel Writers Week* – takes place in County Kerry.

June: *Festival of Music in Great Irish Houses* – classical concerts.

July: *International Folk Dance Festival* – held in Cobh. *Dún Laoghaire Festival* – held in County Dublin; *Galway Arts Festival and horse races; Irish Open Golf Championships*.

August: *Dublin Horse Show* – the top event of the year; *Connemara Pony Show* – held in Clifden, County Galway; *Kilkenny Arts Week; Moynalty Steam Threshing Fair* – held in County Meath; *Oul Lammas Fair*, Ballycastle, County Antrim; *Puck Fair* – three days and nights of non-stop Irish entertainment, Killorglin, County Kerry; *Stradbally Steam Rally* – staged in County Laois.

September: *National Football and Hurling Finals* – Dublin; *Festival of Light Opera* – staged in Waterford; *Rose of Tralee Festival* – an international event.

October: *Kinsale Gourmet Festival* – staged in County Cork; *Dublin Theatre Festival* – new plays by Irish authors and companies from abroad; *Cork International Film Festival; Wexford Opera Festival*, shows of rare operas; *Ballinasloe Fair* (Europe's oldest horse fair), County Galway; *Cork Jazz Festival; Belfast Festival at Queen's*, Ireland's largest arts festival and the highlight of Belfast's calendar for over 40 years.

November: *The International Horse Show* (Dublin) – a major event in the international equestrian calendar.

EATING OUT

Hearty meals are served in a variety of places – from hotels and bars to coffee shops and snack bars, from pubs to restaurants. Pub grub tends to be hot or cold meat pies, sandwiches and simple salads, while restaurants run from the most modest to the truly elegant, with prices to match.

Dublin is increasingly sophisticated in its array and quantity of restaurants, and the city is matching other European capitals as a breeding ground for talented and innovative chefs. It can be expensive, though. Quality French, Italian, Chinese, Indonesian, Indian, Russian and even Cuban cuisines are available throughout Ireland.

Kinsale, a small town in County Cork, has become the gourmet capital of Ireland, but outstanding food can be

A traditional Irish breakfast – not for the faint-hearted

found across the country in the old, remote and often spectacular setting of the estate homes.

The tourist office's *Ireland's Blue Book of Country Houses* and Georgina Campbell's *Jameson Guide* are good sources for exploring these. Don't miss the chance to enjoy a meal at one of Dublin's top restaurants. Lunch prices are usually half the price and may include specials.

You don't have to look far to find an idyllic setting for a picnic in Ireland. Farmhouse cheeses, smoked salmon, fresh baked bread and fresh produce supply the ingredients and the scenery is provided by a long and winding coast, over 400 forest areas and moody mountain views that will seldom let you down even if the weather does.

If you're on a budget, there are many small cafes and tearooms which provide good value. Keep in mind the businessman's lunch, a package deal at many provincial and city restaurants, usually involving a set three courses for a fraction of the cost of an evening meal.

There is also the ever-present chippy. Often the traditional end to a night in the pub, they also make a cheap, tasty and quick option to eating out. Thanks to the long coastline, the fish is always fresh and often made to order.

In addition to VAT (value added tax), a lot of restaurants add a service charge to the bill; extra tips are given at about 10 percent of the total bill.

When to Eat

Breakfast is served from about 7–10am, though in some hotels, matching the general leisurely air, it does not begin until 8am. Lunchtime is from 12.30–2.30pm, give or take half an hour at either end. The time – and name – of the evening meal depends on who and where you are. In rural areas and perhaps the less sophisticated town areas, people dine as early as 6pm. and refer to the evening meal as 'tea'. In the major towns and cities, however, you can have your 'supper' any time from 6 or 7–11pm.

What to Eat

Breakfast

A real Irish breakfast starts the day superlatively. (To others, it may be so filling you find yourself back in the bed of your B&B.)

You'll feel ready for any kind of exertion after a menu of juice, porridge, or cold cereal with milk or cream, fried eggs with bacon and sausages, toast or tasty homemade soda bread, butter, marmalade, tea or coffee.

In Ulster in particular, an important constituent of the breakfast fry-up is fried *farl* (potato bread). Irish soda bread, white or brown, is made from flour and buttermilk, bicarbonate of soda and salt; it's as delicious as cake. Black pudding, a heavy sausage filled with grains and blood, is a treat you'll either love or hate.

Ireland's fresh produce is as tasty as it looks

Other meals

Irish **soups** are usually thick and hearty: vegetables, barley and meat stock with a dab of cream, for instance. Look for potato soup made of potatoes, onions, carrots and parsley.

Fish caught fresh from the Atlantic, the Irish Sea or the island's streams is incredibly good. Keep an eye out for some of these

There's more to wet your whistle than Guinness

great Irish delights: fresh salmon (poached or grilled), smoked salmon, sole and trout from the sea and rivers. Dublin Bay prawns are a big natural resource worthy of their fame, as are Galway oysters (often accompanied by a bottle of stout). With luck you could be offered mussels or lobster, but the great bulk of the catch is usually exported to the Continent.

Meat of the highest quality is at the centre of Irish cuisine. The beef is excellent, but there is very little veal. You'll have a choice of sumptuous steaks (either T-bone, filet mignon or sirloin) or roast beef. Lamb appears as tender chops or as a roast, or the main ingredient in Irish stew, a filling casserole of meat, potatoes, carrots and onions, laced with parsley and thyme. Irish pork products – bacon, sausages, chops and Limerick ham – are also rightly famous. Dublin coddle is a delicious stew of sausages, bacon, onions, potatoes and parsley, a favourite for Saturday night supper in the capital.

Vegetables as basic as the potato play a big part in Irish cooking. Potatoes have been a mainstay of the Irish diet since the 17th century. Mushrooms, which thrive in the cool, humid atmosphere here, are the single biggest horticultural export.

More and more restaurants are now serving vegetarian dishes, and fresh produce from Ireland's farms is a dream come true for those thinking Irish food is nothing more than meat and dairy.

Desserts are often similar to sticky English puddings – trifles, *gâteaux* and generally very sweet offerings, sometimes with a scrumptious topping of thick cream.

What to Drink

A jug of tap water is often found on the table, and for many diners it's the only drink during the meal. Ireland has many

Great care is taken to serve up 'the perfect Guinness'

brands of bottled spring water, widely sold and served in pubs and restaurants, and water is gaining popularity as a substitute for alcoholic drinks, especially at lunchtime.

Wine has become popular in Ireland as links with Europe have strengthened. By a quirk in the law, restaurants licensed to serve sherry and wine cannot

Rural Ireland community centre

serve spirits or beer, but the Irish don't see beer as a dinner accompaniment anyway.

Irish **pubs** are usually as relaxed and friendly as their regular clients. Although the eccentric licensing hours used to mean that public houses in the Republic's urban areas had to close between 2.30 and 3.30pm, this 'holy hour' no longer exists, and most pubs are open all day, but they are still closed on Sunday afternoons. The pubs in Northern Ireland are permitted to open on Sundays, but not all choose to do so.

The Irish drink nearly 500 million pints of **beer** a year, mostly stout – a rich, creamy, dark brown version. Cork's two brands of stout, Beamish and Murphy's, have become increasingly popular. In many a pub the simple order 'a pint, please' means 568 ml of **Guinness**, lovingly drawn from the keg, scraped and topped. The head is so thick that the barman can leave the image of a shamrock sitting within it. A 'glass' of stout means half a pint.

Irish lagers and ales are less filling, and are also worth trying. An interesting Irish drink, **Black Velvet**, combines stout and champagne, and is said to be good for hangovers.

The word **whiskey** comes from the Gaelic *uisce beatha*, 'water of life'. (Purists are at pains to spell Irish whiskey with an 'e' unlike the Scottish version.) Whiskey is matured in wooden casks for at least seven years and is drunk neat, or with a little water – never with ice.

Enthusiasts can visit the world's oldest whiskey distillery, Bushmills <www.bushmills.com>, in Northern Ireland; it has held a licence since 1609. Also, the Old Jameson Distillery is an award-winning destination in Smithfield, the heart of old Dublin, while the Old Midleton Distillery just outside Cork is another option. For further information go to <www.whiskeytours.ie>.

Don't overlook Ireland's generous selection of fresh seafood

Whiskey features in many of Ireland's unusual and delicious drinks: **Irish coffee**, in a stemmed glass, is hot coffee laced with whiskey and sugar, with a tablespoonful of thick cream floating on top.

Two Irish liqueurs merit a try: **Irish mist** – honey and herbs in a whiskey base – tingles on the palate, and **Irish cream liqueur**, in different brands, is also very popular with coffee: there's Bailey's and Carolan's, Sheridan's and St Brendan's. It contains whiskey, chocolate and cream – like a leprechaun's milkshake, they say.

HANDY TRAVEL TIPS

An A–Z Summary of Practical Information

A

ACCOMMODATION (See also CAMPING, YOUTH HOSTELS, and the selection of RECOMMENDED HOTELS starting on *page 127*)

While exploring Ireland you can stay in different types of accommodation: a luxury hotel one night, a family-run guesthouse the next, a farmhouse and a thatched cottage after that. Efficient tourist offices will handle both spur-of-the-moment or long-range reservations for you. The tourist boards are responsible for inspecting and classifying all hostelries, issuing brochures free or at minimal cost, and for listing the various approved establishments available with information about their rates and facilities. Tariffs are government-controlled, and the maximum rate shown in the brochure is the highest which proprietors may charge.

Hotel bills usually include a service charge, and you will find that VAT (value added tax) on the total cost of accommodation, meal and service is included in the rates.

Hotels and motels. These are graded by the tourist authorities into five star ratings.

***** Most luxurious with high standard of cuisine and services.

**** Extremely comfortable with experienced service.

*** Well-furnished, offering a good service; a private bath available but not necessarily in the majority of rooms.

** Well-kept, limited but good cuisine and service.

* Clean and comfortable, hot and cold running water.

Guesthouses. Usually family-run with friendly personal service, these can include full board for resident guests, and are also listed and graded by stars (one to four).

Irish Homes. The Irish Tourist Board issues three informative books: *Be Our Guest, Bed & Breakfast,* and *Irish Farmhouse Holidays,* which cover a full range of hotels, guesthouses and youth hostels, as well as town and country homes and farmhouses. The Northern Ireland Tourist Board publishes similar brochures.

Thatched Cottages. These are available to rent mainly in western Ireland near famous beauty spots in five counties. The details are available from tourist offices or Rent-an-Irish Cottage Ltd, 51 O'Connell Street, Limerick; tel: (061) 411109.

AIRPORTS

International flights arrive at six airports: Dublin, Cork, Kerry, Shannon, Knock and Belfast.

Dublin Airport, situated 11km (7 miles) north of the Republic's capital, is the busiest. Coaches link the airport with Busaras, the city bus terminal, every 20 minutes. There is also a bus to Howth Junction railway station, provided by DART. This is the least expensive option. However you go, the trip takes between half an hour and an hour. Taxi time between the airport and central Dublin is also about half an hour.

Shannon Airport, one of the first Atlantic gateways, is situated about 24km (15 miles) to the west of Limerick. All usual facilities are available, as well as a large and varied duty-free shopping area.

Belfast International Airport (Aldergrove) is 24km (15 miles) west of the city. An bus service to town operates every 30 minutes. **Belfast City Airport** is handily situated near the city's old dockland area.

B

BICYCLE RENTAL (See also MONEY MATTERS)

A network of dealers all over the island encourages bike rental as a way of seeing the real Ireland. Children's and adults' models, racing bikes, and even tandems are all available. Tourist information offices have a leaflet listing dealers in more than 100 towns from Antrim to Cork.

BUDGETING FOR YOUR TRIP

To give you an idea of what to expect, here's a list of average prices in euros with British pounds where applicable.

Accommodation: luxury hotel (double room, bath and breakfast) €100–200 (£70–150). Medium hotel (double room, bath and breakfast) €50–100 (£35–70). Guesthouses (double room with bath) €30-60 (£20–45). In town and country homes and farmhouses, bed and breakfast costs €20-30 (£15–25).

Airport transfer: bus to Dublin €6, AeroDART €5 taxi to central Dublin €20 + tip; bus to Belfast from Aldergrove £6, taxi £20.

Bicycle rental: €45–60 (£30–45) per week, plus deposit.

Buses: local fares €2 (to the most distant suburb). An 8-day out of fifteen bus/rail rambler ticket for unlimited cross-country travel costs €180, an 8-day ticket (bus only) restricted to the Republic of Ireland is €145, a weekly bus ticket for the greater Dublin area costs €17.50. Belfast bus fares range from 70p–£1.40 or £12 for a week.

Camping: €/£10–15 per night.

Car rental (international company): Rentals can begin at $40 per day/ $200 per week (US$) and go to $60 per day/$320 per week with unlimited mileage.Add 12.5 percent tax in the Republic, 17.5% tax in Northern Ireland.

Cigarettes: €4 (£5) per packet of 20.

Entertainment: Movie tickets cost €/£6–9 . Admission to discos and nightclubs are €/£5–15 or more. Theatre tickets are €15–25 (£10-25).

Ferry: Galway–Aran Islands €19 roundtrip.

Meals and drinks: set-price lunch €/£10, dinner €/£15–45; add a carafe of wine at €15 (£10), soft drink €/£2, pint of beer €4 (£2.50), whiskey €/£2.

Museums, stately homes: €/£5 admission.

Taxis: minimum charge, Dublin €5, O'Connell Street to Heuston Station €8, Merrion Square to St Patrick's Cathedral €8. You may find a supplement is payable for extra passengers, baggage, etc.

Tours: Dublin city sightseeing, half-day €12.50. Cork bus tour to the Ring of Kerry €25. Belfast half-day tours £5.

Trains: Dublin–Cork €48.50, Dublin–Cork €31/£22. A 5-day rail explorer ticket for unlimited travel is €106.

C

CAMPING

Officially-approved campsites range from spartan to luxurious, but if a 'no vacancy' sign is posted, take heart: many a farmer will let campers spend the night on his property, but you should always ask first. At some campsites, and at rental agencies, touring caravans (trailers) can be rented. If you're pulling your own, note that the connections for Calor gas tanks are not suitable for the cylinders sold in Ireland. Lists of camping and caravanning parks and their various facilities are available from tourist information offices or the Irish Caravan and Camping Council, PO Box 4443, Dublin 2 <www.campingireland.ie>. Contact the Northern Ireland Tourist Board at 59 North Street, Belfast BT1 1NB; tel: (028) 9023 1221 <www.discovernorthernireland.com>.

Horse-drawn caravans may be rented by the week if you want to get a taste of the gipsy life. They are most commonly found in the west and southwest of Ireland. Bookings should be made in advance through the Central Reservation Service, Irish Tourist Board, Baggot Street Bridge, Dublin 2; tel: (01) 602 4000; <www.ireland.travel.ie>.

CAR RENTAL (See also DRIVING IN IRELAND)

Dozens of car rental companies operate at airports and in the towns. The internationally known firms usually have slightly higher rates than their local competitors, but you may find that booking from abroad might get you better value for money. Some companies permit cars to be picked up in one place and returned elsewhere.

Most companies have a two-tiered tariff, raising prices by up to 10 to 20 percent for the summer season. In any season, cars may be rented on either a time-plus-mileage basis or with unlimited mileage, but if you're unsure whether you'll be chalking up enough travelling to justify the unlimited rate, the firm may agree to let you choose the more favourable tariff retroactively. Investigate before you travel.

A valid national licence, normally at least two years old, will be required. Many firms permit 21-year-old drivers to rent cars, but the minimum age can be as high as 25. The maximum age, depending on the company, ranges from 65 to 70. Credit cards are accepted in lieu of a deposit.

Rental rates include third-party liability insurance. Additional coverage can be arranged on the spot, and comprehensive coverage is recommended.

Don't forget: drive on the left and wear your seat belt at all times.

CLIMATE AND CLOTHING

The Gulf Stream is credited with keeping the Irish weather mild year-round, but the unexpected can happen with readings as cold as -19°C (-2°F) and as hot as 33°C (92°F) recorded over the past century. May is usually the sunniest month of the year, and December the dullest. Average monthly temperatures in Dublin:

	J	F	M	A	M	J	J	A	S	O	N	D
°F	41	41	43	47	51	56	59	58	56	50	45	43
°C	5	5	6	8	11	13	15	14	13	10	7	6

Temperatures do not vary much from north to south, but the weather in the west and southwest can be a good deal wetter than elsewhere because the winds come in over the land direct from the sea, bringing moisture with them. It may be wise, therefore, to pack some light protective clothing for the summer, and certainly warmer items in the winter.

In the winter the Wicklow Mountains near Dublin, Donegal in the northwest and County Kerry in the southwest have heavy snowfalls, making the territory dangerous even for the most seasoned walkers and climbers. Therefore wear hardy, warm and protective clothing and follow the proper code by informing the hotel owners of your route and time of return – and take some provisions with you.

COMMUNICATIONS

Post Offices. The Post operates all mail services offered in the Republic. Most mailboxes are pillar-shaped (a few antiques still have Queen Victoria's monogram on them), and are painted green. Most post offices are open from 9am–5.30pm, but the main one – the historic General Post Office in O'Connell Street, Dublin – is open 8am–8pm Mon–Sat, and 10.30am– 6.30pm on Sun. Postcard shops and newsstands sometimes sell stamps too. In some areas a post office may be identified by a sign in Irish only – *Oifig an Phoist*.

If you don't know where you'll be staying, you can have mail sent to you poste restante (general delivery) to any town. Letters sent poste restante to the GPO in Dublin may be collected up to 8pm.

In Northern Ireland the mailboxes are red. Note that Republic of Ireland stamps may not be used on mail posted in Northern Ireland and British stamps are invalid in the Republic.

Telephones. Public telephones are found in post offices, hotels, stores and on the street. In the Republic sentry-box booths – cream with green trim – and modern aluminium and glass booths are increasingly used. They are marked in Gaelic, *Telefon*.

Instructions for operating coin telephones are usually given. Payphones in Ireland use 10¢, 20¢, 50¢ and €1 coins for direct dialling of local, national and international calls. Many payphones use calling cards, which can be bought from local post offices and shops. Operator assistance is available by dialing 10.

In Northern Ireland, public telephones are found in metal and glass booths or yellow cubicles. They operate with 10p, 20p, 50p, £1and £2 coins as well as phonecards. Do not deposit money until the connection has been made; a series of rapid beeps will indicate when the machine is ready to accept your coins.

CRIME (See also EMERGENCIES and POLICE)

The Crime Prevention Office of the Garda Siochana (police) warns visitors to carry a minimum of cash and jewellery. Pickpockets do operate in shops and public places. Tourists who leave property un-attended risk losses. Park in well-lit, busy areas and keep valuables out of sight. Thefts from hotel rooms are rare.

CUSTOMS AND ENTRY FORMALITIES

Citizens of many countries do not require visas. British travellers directly from Britain require no photo identity only, but others should present valid documents. Visitors from countries infected with yellow fever will need proof of vaccinations. It is forbidden to import pornographic material or books listed by the Republic of Ireland government's censor. You may bring unlimited European currency into either country, but you may only take out up to €100, unless travelling to another euro-zone country. Foreign currency brought in can be taken out, plus the equivalent of €500 (travellers' cheques excluded). This does not apply to people travelling between Ireland and Great Britain, the Channel Islands, or the Isle of Man.

Residents of European countries with non-tax free goods bought in the EU can bring into the Republic 800 cigarettes or 200 cigars or 1kg of tobacco, plus 1.5 litres of spirits and 5 litres of wine. European residents with tax-free goods can bring in 200 cigarettes or 50 cigars or 250g tobacco plus 10 litres of spirits and 90 litres of wine. Residents of non-European countries can bring in 200 cigarettes or 50 cigars or 250g tobacco, plus 1 litre of spirits and 2 litres of wine.

The customs restrictions between the Republic and Northern Ireland are normally limited to animals and agricultural products. Most of the previously unauthorised or blocked border crossings have been reinstated, and there are seldom any security checks.

D

DRIVING IN IRELAND (See also CAR RENTAL and EMERGENCIES)

Traffic moves on the left. Beware: some road-signs are in Gaelic only. **Importing your car.** Be sure to have the registration papers and insurance coverage. The usual formula for UK drivers is the Green Card, which is an extension to the normal insurance, making it valid in other countries. Virtually any valid driving licence from any country is recognised in Ireland.

Driving conditions. If you're not accustomed to driving on the left, be careful for the first few days, especially when turning corners and at roundabouts. Driving on country lanes can be a pleasurable experience, but be alert for the unexpected: you could find cattle camped in the road, tractors inching along, and ambling pedestrians blocking your way. On zebra crossings (marked by amber beacons), pedestrians have the right of way. Beware of bicycles weaving in and out of town traffic; cyclists make their own rules here.

Speed limits. Unless otherwise marked, the speed limit in the Irish Republic is 96km/h (60mph) on the open road, and it is set at 48 or 64km/h (30 or 40mph) in towns and built-up areas. On motorways the limit is 112km/h (70mph). In Northern Ireland the limit in towns is 48km/h (30mph), 96km/h (60mph) in the country, and 112km/h (70mph) on motorways.

Parking. This is becoming more difficult, especially in Dublin and other big cities. Some towns have zones requiring discs or other variations on this time-limit system. Check the signs for the regulations that apply.

If you leave your car on a yellow line during business hours you may be fined for parking in a no-parking zone. If you leave your car on a double line, meaning no waiting (regardless of time of day), it may be towed away, and you will have to pay a fine plus towing charges.

Fuel. In some areas finding a petrol station open on a Sunday may be a problem, so it's best to top up on Saturday for weekend excursions. Petrol (gas) is sold by the litre.

Seat belts. Drivers and front-seat passengers must wear seat belts in the Republic and Northern Ireland; failure to use them may be punished by a fine. If a vehicle is built with rear seat belts, it is compulsory to use them.

Drinking and driving. Police on both sides of the border are strict about this. Any driver suspected of being affected by drink will be subjected to a roadside breathaliser test. Those who fail – and it only takes a pint or two of beer – risk heavy fines or jail or both. The crackdown affects visitors as well as residents.

Road signs. Many international picture-signs are used on highways. The road direction signs in the Republic are mostly in English and Gaelic, but in Irish-speaking enclaves the English may be omitted. Traditional road signs give distances in miles and, increasingly, in kilometres.

Some signs may not be comprehensible to visitors:

In Ireland	*In the US*
Clearway	No parking along highway
Cul de sac	Dead end
Dual carriageway	Divided highway
Layby	Rest area
Level crossing	Rail crossing
Loose chippings	Loose gravel
No overtaking	No passing
Road up	Under construction
Roadworks	Men working
Soft edges (or **margin**)	Soft shoulder

E

ELECTRIC CURRENT

The standard current everywhere is 220v, 50AC, but you will find that hotels usually have special sockets for shavers, running at both 220 and 110v.

Note that it is possible for certain appliances to need a converter, and also that adapter plugs may be required to fit into Ireland's two types of wall outlets. These can be either three-pin flat or two-pin round.

EMBASSIES AND CONSULATES

The Dublin telephone directory lists foreign embassies and consular services under the heading 'Diplomatic and Consular Missions'. Consular agencies in provincial towns are all listed in Part 2 of the directory under the same heading.

The details of the principal embassies and consulates in **Dublin** are as follows:

Australia: Fitzwilton House, Wilton Terrace, Dublin 2; tel: (01) 664 5300; <www.australianembassy.ie>.

Canada: 65 St Stephen's Green, Dublin 2; tel: (01) 417 4100; e-mail <cdnembsy@iol.ie>.

Great Britain: 29 Merrion Road, Dublin 4; tel: (01) 205 3700; <www.britishembassy.ie>.

US: 42 Elgin Road, Dublin 4; tel: (01) 668 7122; <www.usembassy.ie>.

In Northern Ireland:

US: Queen's House, 14 Queen Street, Belfast BT1 6EQ; tel: (028) 9032 8239; <www.usembassy.org.uk/nireland/>.

EMERGENCIES (See also EMBASSIES and CONSULATES and MEDICAL CARE)

To contact the police, fire department, or an ambulance in an emergency, dial **999** from any telephone in the Republic or Northern Ireland (no coin required), and tell the emergency operator which service you need. Have details of your location ready before you make your call.

G

GAY AND LESBIAN TRAVELLERS

Nowadays the general attitude of younger people in Ireland tends to be tolerant towards gays and lesbians, but some travellers may find there is a slightly more socially conservative attitude in the southern parts of Ireland and some of the more provincial or remote areas of the country.

Various organisations provide advisory services for gay people. They include the Gay Federation/Gay Community News, Dublin; tel: (01) 671 0939; <www.gcn.ie> and the **Gay Switchboard,** Dublin; tel: (01) 872-1055; open 8–10pm Sun to Fri, and 3.30–6.30pm Sat. And the **Lesbian Line,** Dublin; tel: (01) 872-9911. Open 7–9pm Thur.

GETTING THERE

It is advisable to consult a travel agent for the latest information as well as writing to the local tourist offices for information in advance.

FROM GREAT BRITAIN

By Air

Visitors and tourists can fly in from airports across the UK to Dublin, Shannon, Cork, Kerry, Waterford and Knock in the Republic and to Belfast International, Belfast City and Derry airports in Northern Ireland. New routes are opening all the time, so it may be worth checking with the airline of your choice for information on the most convenient connections.

Charter Flights and Package Tours. A wide array of packages is currently available for visitors, making good use of the varied accommodation Ireland has to offer.

Some airlines offer fly-drive tours, as well as special fares which may include your flight and all the transport to and from your final destination in Ireland. Check with the airline of your choice.

By Sea

Passenger and car ferries sail frequently from Holyhead to Dublin and Dún Laoghaire. There is also a regular service from Fishguard and Pembroke to Rosslare Harbour, and from Swansea to Cork. Ferries shuttle several times a day from Cairnryan and Stranraer to Larne (near Belfast). A daily catamaran service runs between Stranraer and Belfast.

Those touring Ireland without a car might want to buy a Rambler or Rover ticket that allows 5, 8 or 15 days bus travel. The latter is also valid in Northern Ireland. The Irish Explorer allows you up to 15 days of bus and rail travel excluding Northern Ireland on just the one ticket. These can be bought either at home or in Ireland from *Bus Éireann* <www.buseireann.ie> or *Iarnród Éireann-Irish Rail*. InterRail Passes are valid for 15 or 30 days in Europe for those under 26 and for senior citizens over 65.

FROM NORTH AMERICA

By Air

Travellers from almost every major American city and several major Canadian cities can make connections to Dublin, Shannon or Belfast through New York or Boston. Regular services are also available to Knock.

Charter Flights and Package Tours. Charter flights to Shannon, with connections to Dublin, feature even further air-fare reductions. The tourist boards have full details of charter flights.

GUIDES AND TOURS

Guided tours are conducted at some major attractions as part of the admission fee, and a variety of excursions are led by guides, covering major monuments and beauty spots by bus. Tourist offices have schedules; the Dublin office has a list of qualified guides.

L

LANGUAGE

English is spoken with lilting Irish accents everywhere in Ireland. In the Gaeltacht areas of the west and south, the principal language is Irish, though most people speak fluent English too. Bilingualism is officially encouraged in the Republic. Summer courses in the Irish language are given in the Gaeltacht. Write to Comhdhail Naisiunta na Gaeilge, 86 Sraid Gardner Iocht, Baile Atha Cliath 1, Republic of Ireland.

Here is a short Irish glossary to help you read the signs:

Irish/Gaelic	*English*
ar(d)	high place

áth	ford of river
baile, bally	hamlet, group of houses, town
beann, ben	mountain peak
cairn	mound of stones on top of a prehistoric tomb
carrick, carrig	rock
cather	fort
clachan, clochan	small group of dwellings; stepping stones across a river; beehive-shaped hut
clon, cluain	meadow
corrach	marsh or low plain
corrie	circular hollow with steep sides
currach	small boat
derry, dare	oak tree or wood
donagh	church
drum, drom	ridge, hillock
dun, doon	fort
ennis, inch, innis(h)	island
keel, kill, caol	narrow
kil, kill, cill	church; monk's cell
lough	lake, sea inlet
mol, mull	height
ros	promontory or wood
sceillig, skellig	crag, rock
sliabh, slieve	mountain
tulach, tully	hillock

And here are a few phrases to help you in general, with a rough guide to pronunciation:

Dia dhuit	hello	*diah guich*

slán	goodbye	*slawn*

(many people in Ireland also say 'good luck' meaning 'goodbye')

oiche mhaith	good night	*e-ha wah*
go raibh maith agat	thank you	*goh rev moh a-gut*
le do thoil	please	*leh doh hol*
tá fáilte romhat	you're welcome	*taw faltcha rowet*
sláinte!	cheers!	*sloyn-tcha*
gam pardún	excuse me	*gum par-doon*
Cá bhuil an ... ?	Where is the ... ?	*koh will on*

LOST PROPERTY

The first place to go in search of lost property is the local police station. However, public transport organizations sometimes have their own lost property departments. For items you may have left by accident on trains or buses in Dublin, try the Dublin Bus Lost Property Office, tel: (01) 703 1321, or the Irish Rail Lost Property, Connolly Station, Amiens Street, Dublin 1.

The main lost property office in Belfast is at Musgrave Street c/o the RUC (Royal Ulster Constabulary) Police Station; tel: (028) 9065 0222.

M

MEDIA

Radio and Television. In the Republic, state-run Radio Telefís Éireann (RTE) is the largest broadcaster, though cable television has expanded the choice and includes standard British stations. Most programmes are in English except for a few Irish or bilingual ones. Some foreign films are shown in the original language with English subtitles. RTE operates three radio stations mainly in English, as well as Raidio na Gaeltachta with an all-Irish programme. In Northern Ireland, the BBC runs five radio stations and two TV stations alongside ITV and Channel Four.

Transistors and car radios can pick up the principal radio stations of Europe; reception is best at night.

Newspapers. Two national morning papers are published in Dublin – the *Irish Independent* and the *Irish Times*. The *Cork Examiner* is also considered a national daily.

Northern Ireland has two morning dailies, the *News Letter* and the *Irish News*. Entertainment news is covered in the *Evening Herald* of Dublin, the *Evening Echo* of Cork and the *Belfast Telegraph*. Sunday papers are also useful, and visitors will also find a what's on section in the fortnightly magazine *In Dublin*.

Irish editions of Britain's national daily and Sunday newspapers are sold almost everywhere in both countries on the morning of publication. Leading newsagents in the major towns also sell European newspapers and magazines as well as American magazines.

MEDICAL CARE (See also EMERGENCIES)

Residents of EU countries are covered by reciprocal health care in the Republic and in Northern Ireland, and visitors from mainland Europe should ensure that they bring a completed E111 form; no form is required for UK visitors. Other nationalities should have some form of hospital insurance – many package tours provide temporary policies.

Hotels usually know which local doctors are available, but in an emergency you can dial **999** to find a doctor on call.

The Dental Hospital, 20 Lincoln Place, Dublin 2; tel: (01) 612 7200, takes dental emergency cases from 9–11am and 2–4pm.

Pharmacies (chemists) operate during shopping hours. A few stay open until 10pm; in Belfast many are open on Sundays, while in the Republic only some are open 11am–1pm.

MONEY MATTERS

Currency. The unit of currency used in the Irish Republic is the euro (€); in Northern Ireland the British pound sterling (£) is used. Both are divided into 100 units. These units are called cents in the Republic, pence in the north. Banks everywhere on the island are accustomed to exchanging euro and pounds. Euro banknotes are issued in €5, €10,

€20, €50, €100 and also €500 denominations. Coins come in 1, 2, 5, 10, 20 and 50 cents and 1 and 2 euro.

Exchange facilities. All major banks and many building societies provide exchange facilities. Major post offices, including the GPO in Dublin, have a bureau de change. Some international travel agencies also change money and travellers' cheques. Be sure to take along your passport as proof of identity when cashing travellers' cheques (see also OPENING HOURS for further information).

The O'Connell Street Tourist Information Office in Dublin and the Cork Office in Grand Parade operate money exchange services. The Dublin office will change your money from 9am–5.15pm Monday to Friday, while the Cork office provides this facility from 9am–1.15pm and 2.30–5.15pm Mon to Fri.

Credit cards and travellers' cheques are widely accepted in Irish shops, hotels, restaurants and car-rental firms. Cash points at banks throughout the island offer cash advances on major cards.

O

OPENING HOURS

The opening hours of shops and offices can vary from season to season and according to where they are located.

Shops in the cities are normally open from 9am–5.30pm Mon to Sat; country towns have one early closing day. However, the big shopping centres often stay open until 9pm on Thur and Fri. Smaller shops, particularly groceries and newsstands, often open on Sun and many stay open until 11pm.

Offices and businesses mostly operate from 9am–5.30pm Mon to Fri. Tourist information offices are open from 10am–6pm with longer summer hours in the busiest places.

Banks. In general banks are open 10am–4pm Mon to Fri in the Republic. Most towns have a late opening day once a week (Thur in Dublin), when banks stay open until 5pm. You'll also find that many banks remain open over the lunch hour. In Northern Ireland banks are open from 10am–3.30pm. Outside Belfast, branches may close for lunch.

The bank at Dublin Airport is open every day of the year except Christmas, from 6.45am–9pm in the winter and until 10pm in the summer.

Pubs. Licensing hours have been streamlined. In the Republic, the winter hours are 10.30am–11.30pm, with an extra half hour in summer. On Sun all year, pubs are open from 12.30–2pm and from 4–11pm. In addition, there is half-an-hour drinking-up time in the evenings all year round. In Northern Ireland, pubs are open Mon to Sat 11.30am–11pm, all year. Sun opening is a relatively new departure, and is followed by some pubs, which now open from 12.30–2.30pm, and from 7–10pm, all year. In addition, there is half-an-hour drinking-up time.

Museums, stately homes, etc. Museums and stately homes follow no general rule except that visiting hours will often be curtailed in winter. There are no universal days when these institutions are closed, though Sun, Mon, or Tue are the most probable. To avoid disappointment always check first with the nearest tourist information office.

P

PHOTOGRAPHY

Be sure to ask permission before you take photos in museums and historic churches; sometimes flashbulbs are forbidden. Military bases are off-limits to photographers. Please note that in Northern Ireland you should avoid pointing your camera, or anything else, at personnel or installations of the security forces.

POLICE (See also EMERGENCIES)

The civic guard (police force) of the Irish Republic is the Garda Siochana, known as the Garda (pronounced 'gorda'). The Police Service of Northern Ireland performs similar duties in the North. In case of emergency, telephone 999, in both the Republic and Northern Ireland.

PUBLIC HOLIDAYS

Shops, banks, official departments and restaurants are closed on public holidays. If a date falls on a Sunday, then the following Monday is taken in lieu.

In the Republic of Ireland and Northern Ireland:

1 January	*New Year's Day*
17 March	*St. Patrick's Day*
March/April (movable date)	*Good Friday/Easter Monday*
25 December	*Christmas Day*
26 December	*Boxing Day*

In the Republic of Ireland only:

first Monday in June	*June Bank Holiday*
last Monday in August	*August Bank Holiday*
last Monday in October	*October Bank Holiday*

In Northern Ireland only:

first Monday in May	*May Day*
last Monday in May	*Spring Bank Holiday*
12 July	*Orangemen's Day*
last Monday in August	*Summer Bank Holiday*

R

RELIGION

About 95 percent of the people in the Irish Republic are Catholic. Many go to Sunday Mass, which can be heard in Dublin almost any time, from 6am–9pm, in English, and sometimes in Irish.

Dublin's cathedrals are of the (Anglican) Church of Ireland, and schedules of the services at these and other Protestant churches can be found in hotels, and in Saturday papers. Dublin has Protestant, Greek Orthodox, Jewish and Islamic places of worship.

In Northern Ireland, Catholics make up around a third of the population, but they outnumber the largest single Protestant group, the Presbyterians, as well as the Church of Ireland.

The ecclesiastic capital of Ireland is Armagh, situated in the North with two cathedrals, one Catholic and the other Church of Ireland. Both are called St Patrick's.

T

TIME DIFFERENCES

Ireland sets its clocks one hour ahead of GMT from mid-March to the end of October, but the rest of the year the clocks are set to GMT.

TIPPING

Most hotels and restaurants include a service charge, so tipping is unnecessary. If not, 10 percent of the bill in a restaurant or a couple of euro a day for cleaners is expected in the Republic. In Nothern Ireland the service charge is around 12 percent. In either country, taxis are usually tipped by simply rounding up the fare.

TOILETS

Public conveniences abound in Irish towns, and are well sign-posted. The only hitch is that the gender signs on doors in the Republic may be printed in Gaelic, not English. *Mná* should not be misconstrued as a misprint for men; it's Gaelic for ladies. *Fir* means gentlemen.

TOURIST INFORMATION OFFICES

Tourist information offices all over Ireland provide full travel information and advice, booklets, maps and a comprehensive hotel reservation service (for a small charge), which can extend to booking novel horse-drawn caravans and self-drive cabin cruisers. The offices are usually open from 10am–6pm, although many local ones operate only in the summer. For enquiries, write to one of the following:

Irish Tourist Board, Bord Fáilte, Baggot Street Bridge, Baggot Street, Dublin 2; tel: (01) 602 4000; <www.ireland.travel.ie>.

Northern Ireland Tourist Board, St Anne's Court, 59 North Street, Belfast BT1 INB; tel: (028) 9023 1221; <www.discover northernireland.com>.

You may also address your enquiries to offices of the **British Tourist Authority** the world over, <www.visitbritain.com>.

TRANSPORT (See also MONEY MATTERS)

Buses. The state-run Bus Éireann operates an extensive network of local, provincial and express bus routes, including full cross-border services in conjunction with Northern Ireland's Ulsterbus Ltd. The service to the various destinations of tourist interest is increased in the summer. You can buy a handy, pocket-sized timetable at bus stations and tourist information offices. *Bus Atha Cliath/Dublin Bus* runs Dublin Area Services. A separate book lists all bus and train routes in the Dublin district.

The bus services cover almost every town and village. Expressway buses provide a non-stop inter-city service, while the so-called Provincial vehicles make frequent stops in rural areas.

Iarnród Éireann-Irish Rail and *Bus Éireann* sell rambler tickets allowing unlimited cross-country travel for up to 15 days. There is also an overlander ticket with 15 days of unlimited travel in the Republic, and with Ulsterbus and Northern Ireland Railways.

On some buses the destination is indicated in Irish only, so if you don't want to arrive in Gaillimh (Galway) instead of Gleann Garb (Glengarriff), you'd better learn the correct Gaelic name before you start out. You will find that the timetable book has a useful glossary.

The busiest bus routes in the cities use double-deckers, in which you pay the driver as you enter. Queues are taken seriously. The line should face the direction from which the bus will arrive, except where the bus stop sign indicates otherwise.

Trains. Passenger train lines in the Republic have been cut back to the main routes, but cross-country services to and from Dublin are both quick and comfortable. The main inter-city routes have air-conditioned, sound-proofed expresses.

There are two classes on through-trains: Standard (2nd class) and Super Standard (1st class). *Iarnród Éireann-Irish Rail* sells a 5-day rail ticket and an 8-day bus/rail ticket for unlimited travel in the Republic, and a 15-day bus/rail pass valid in Northern Ireland too. Train timetables are on sale at railway stations and tourist offices.

Note: Dublin has two main-line railway stations (Heuston and Connolly), as well as a commuter-line station, so be sure to check in advance for the correct terminal.

Some trip times on express trains:

Dublin–Belfast:	2hr 10 minutes
Dublin–Cork:	2hr 30 minutes
Dublin–Galway:	2hr 50 minutes
Dublin–Waterford:	2hr 35 minutes

Ireland has now joined the group of countries which are honouring the **Eurailpass**, a flat-rate unlimited mileage ticket, valid for rail travel in Western Europe outside the UK. The **Eurail Youthpass** is similar to the Eurailpass, but offers second-class travel at a cheaper rate to anyone under 26. This ticket is available to visitors from outside Europe.

Taxis. Irish taxis may be found cruising the streets, but most park at designated stands waiting for clients. Taxis can also be contacted by telephone (see the classified telephone directory under *Taxicabs – Ranks and Shelters*).

Many towns have radio-dispatched taxis, but these usually charge extra for the mileage to pick up the client. Fares can vary from town to town. Dublin and Cork have metered taxis while smaller towns have standard fares or charges by agreement.

Very few Dublin taxi drivers have been known to add imaginary supplements to the fare. Note that you should pay only the charge on the meter plus, if applicable, supplements for extra passengers, additional luggage, waiting time, and trips on public holidays or after midnight.

Radio-cab dispatchers in Dublin can be reached on any of the following numbers; tel: 676 1111, 668 3333 and 677 2222.

Boats and Ferries. With over 4,800km (3,000 miles) of coastline and 14,480km (9,000 miles) of rivers and streams, Ireland is a boater's paradise. You might rent a fishing boat to take advantage of the excellent fresh-water and sea fishing, or enjoy the country's scenic splendours in a rented cruiser (normally available with two to eight berths).

No boating permit is needed for travelling on the Shannon, and all companies offer a free piloting lesson. Points of departure include Carrick-on-Shannon, Athlone, Banagher and Killaloe.

The rugged islands off the coast of Ireland are rich in folklore, antiquities and eye-catching natural wonders (especially birdlife). The Irish Tourist Board issues an information sheet – *Island Boat Services* – listing numerous possibilities, including scheduled ferries. The Aran Islands are only a 20-km (30-mile) steamer ride from Galway; and crossings can also be made from Rossaveal, May to September and from Doolin in County Clare. If you wish to visit the islands in a rented boat, check that it's registered, which will mean it will have adequate insurance coverage.

There are connections by air, as well, which are around 20 minutes. Garinish Island, which is noted for its exuberant vegetation, is only 10 minutes away from Glengarriff (County Cork). Bad weather may interrupt ferry services.

TRAVELLERS WITH DISABILITIES

A lot of progress has been made in recent years to provide more facilities for travellers with disabilities. Ramps have been provided, giving access to many community buildings, and much of the public transport system has been geared up to welcoming people with disabilities.

The more modern city buses in Dublin have facilities for wheelchair users to board the bus, and trains have level entry access. Airlines are also friendly towards passengers with disabilities. For advice and information, contact the **National Council for the Blind in Dublin**, tel: (01) 830 7033, and the **National Chaplaincy for the Deaf**, also in Dublin, tel: (01) 830 5744.

W

WOMEN TRAVELLERS

Women travelling alone in Ireland need to be as cautious as they are in their own home countries, particularly in the main cities. To ensure your safety, take a friend with you if possible, or decide to travel through dark and quiet areas by taxi. Inform yourself in advance about the times of the last trains, buses, etc., and have enough funds with you to pay for the full cost of your return travel by taxi, if necessary. Also, take some relevant telephone numbers with you for taxis, the police, and some advisory organisations.

In Dublin, the area north of the River Liffey and west of the city centre is best avoided at night if you are alone. Similarly, the centres of Cork and Limerick are best avoided at night by women travelling on their own.

Y

YOUTH HOSTELS

The Irish Youth Hostels Association runs 50 hostels in the Republic of Ireland. Membership cards are required, and these are issued by national youth hostel associations overseas.

An official handbook is available from the **Irish Youth Hostels Association (HO)**, 61 Mountjoy Street, Dublin 7; tel: (01) 830 4555; <www.irelandyha.org>.

There are a dozen youth hostels in Northern Ireland. Details can be requested from **Youth Hostel Information**, 22–32 Donegall Road, Belfast BT12 5JN; tel: (028) 9031 5435; <www.hini.org.uk>.

Recommended Hotels

A wide variety of accommodation can be found in Northern Ireland and the Republic. Bed and breakfast can cost as little as €15 (£10) per night. For €40 (£30) a night, hotels can be luxurious. Those registered with Bord Fáilte, the Irish Tourist Board, have guaranteed standards. Some hotels, like Ashford Castle, Dromoland Castle and Waterford Castle offer luxury at €300–600 per night. Self-catering accommodation is widespread, though you will have to book well in advance during the peak summer months. The international star system awards top hotels 5 stars and 1 star to modest hotels. Guesthouses get 1 to 4 stars. Local tourist information offices have details of offers in their area. Hotel prices are subject to 12½ percent VAT in the Republic; 17½ percent in Northern Ireland.

Price categories for a double room in high season:

€€€	over €200/£150
€€	€100–200/£80–150
€	under €100/£80

DUBLIN

Blooms Hotel € *6 Anglesea Street, Dublin 2; tel: 671 5622; fax: 671 5997, <www.blooms.ie>*. Located in the Temple Bar area, and like most hotels here, there's a stylish restaurant, bar and basement nightclub to keep you entertained most of the night.

Buswells Hotel €€ *Molesworth Street, Dublin 2; tel: 614 6500; fax: 676 2090, <www.quinnhotels.com>*. Centrally located just opposite the National Museums complex, Buswells is set in a former Georgian townhouse and a favourite haunt of Dublin politicians. Most come just for the restaurant and bar.

Central Hotel €–€€ *1–5 Exchequer Street, Dublin 2; tel: 679 7302; fax: 679 7303; <www.centralhotel.ie>*. Around for over one

-hundred years and housed in a comfortable, refurbished Victorian building with a location as central as its name.

Clarence Hotel €€€ *6-8 Wellington Quay, Dublin 2; tel: 407 0800; fax: 407 0820; <www.theclarence.ie>*. Once upon a time this was simply a happy home for clergy up from the country on business. Now it's owned by U2 members and its Octagon bar is one of the most popular meeting places in Dublin. The hotel itself is decked out with Irish craftmanship that's contemporary yet reminiscient of that country past.

Conrad Dublin €€€ *Earlsfort Terrace, Dublin 2; tel: 602 8900; fax: 676 5424; <www.conraddublin.ie>*. Situated just off St Stephen's Green, the Conrad is the first stop for travelling royalty, though the service seems to roll out the red carpet for all guests. It's most popular for business people but the pub attracts Dubliners.

Davenport Hotel €€€ *Merrion Square, Dublin 2; tel: 607 3500; fax: 661 5663; <www.davenporthotel.ie>*. An elegant lemon-coloured building dating from the 1860s and set amidst the attractions of Merrion Square.

Dublin International Youth Hostel € *61 Mountjoy Street, Dublin 7; tel: 830 4555; fax: 830 5808; <www.irelandyha.org>*. Budget-priced accommodation in a converted convent.

Le Meridien Shelbourne Hotel €€€ *27 St Stephen's Green, Dublin 2; tel: 663 4500; fax: 661 6006; <wwwshelbourne.ie>*. Once home to the Irish Constitution (it was written here), it is now home to Dublin's more distinguished visitors. You couldn't ask for more than a room overlooking St Stephen's Green, but the popularity of the Horseshoe Bar with Dublin's gliterati will give you even more to look at.

Longfield's Hotel €€ *9/10 Fitzwilliam Street, Dublin 2; tel: 676 1367; fax: 676 1542; <www.longfields.ie>*. In an excellent location, this is the cosy house you wish you could afford in Dublin. It's furnished with antiques and inhabits two splendid

Georgian buildings between Merrion and Fitzwilliam squares. There's also a first-class restaurant.

Mont Clare Hotel €€–€€€ *Merrion Square, Dublin 2; tel: 607 3800; fax: 661 5663; <www.ocallaghanhotels.ie>.* Just a few doors down from the National Gallery, this refurbished hotel still sports the Gallery Bar downstairs – a mahogany bar with old stained-glass windows.

Royal Dublin Hotel €€–€€€ *40 Upper O'Connell Street, Dublin 1; tel: 873 3666; fax: 873 3120; <www.royaldublin.com>.* Convenient central location near Parnell Square. A modern hotel with an old world ambience, located in Dublin's oldest Georgian house from 1752. Restaurant and bars.

Staunton's on the Green Guesthouse € *83 St Stephen's Green, South Dublin 2; tel: 478 2300; fax: 478 2263; <www.stauntons.net>.* Exclusive Georgian house overlooking the green with period decor.

The Westbury €€–€€€ *Grafton Street, Dublin 2; tel: 679 1122; fax: 679 7078; <www.jurysdoyle.com>.* A luxury city centre hotel that knows best how to cater to business visitors, though with this location leisure visitors will never need walk far to the city's attractions.

Wynn's Hotel €€ *35–39 Lower Abbey Street, Dublin 1; tel: 874 5131; fax: 874 1556; <www.wynnshotel.ie>.* This city centre hotel is just around the corner from the Abbey Theatre.

CORK

Blue Haven Hotel € *3 Pearse Street, Kinsale; tel: (021) 477 2209; fax: (021) 477 4268; <www.bluehavenkinsale.com>.* Individually-styled rooms are well-planned but compact, with the type of space you'd expect in a city centre hotel. There is a fine wine bar and coffee shop to retire to, though, and the location couldn't be better. Full Irish breakfast included.

Forte Travelodge € *Blackash, Kinsale Road Roundabout, South Ring Road, Cork; tel: (021) 431 0722 or 1 800 709709; fax: (021) 431 0723; <www.travelodge.co.uk>.* Well-run, modestly-priced modern family hotel.

Quality Hotel & Leisure Centre Cork € *John Redmond Street, Cork; tel: (021) 455 1793; fax: (021) 455 1665; <www.choicehotels ireland.ie>.* Located in a historic building at the heart of the city. Large, well-equipped bedrooms and a leisure centre, Club Vitae, featuring 20-m pool, steam room, sauna, children's pool and fully-equipped gymnasium.

GALWAY

Galway Great Southern Hotel €€–€€€ *Eyre Square, Galway; tel: (091) 564041; fax: (091) 566704; <www.gshotels.com>.* Historic 19th-century railway hotel located in the heart of the city. There's no lack of old Irish charm here but the facilities are modern, up-to-date and comfortable. O'Flaherty's Pub in the basement gives you the traditional Irish experience, the cocktail lounge offers a more modern one.

KERRY

Benners Hotel €–€€ *County Kerry, Main Street, Dingle; tel: (066) 915 1638; fax: (066) 915 1412; <www.dinglebenners.com>.* Comfortable hotel that's been a town centre fixture for over 300 years. Get one of the older bedrooms if you can. Though a bit nosier they offer more charm than the newer rooms.

Doyles Seafood Bar and Town House € *John Street, Dingle; tel: (066) 915 1174; fax: (066) 915 1816; <www.doylesofdingle.com>.* One of several restaurants in Ireland which serves such delicious food they thoughtfully provide a guesthouse so that diners can stick around for breakfast. People mostly come here for the local seafood served in the characterful restaurant. But the eight rooms on offer are just as cosy and there's little doubt about the quality of the breakfast.

Sheen Falls Lodge €€–€€€ *Kenmare; tel: (064) 41600; fax: (064) 41386; <www.sheenfallslodge.ie>*. A 120-hectare (300-acre) estate and waterside setting comes along with a room in this lodge. The lounge bar welcomes you in with a roaring fire and gives you a view of the spilling waterfall outside. Spacious rooms offer views of the river or Kenmare Bay. There is also an equestrian centre, library and nature walk through the woodland.

KILKENNY

Club House Hotel € *Patrick Street, Kilkenny; tel: (056) 772 1994; fax: (056) 777 1920; <www.clubhousehotel.com>*. Historic 18th-century hotel; mementoes include a set of witty 19th-century political cartoons. Full Irish breakfast included.

Foulksrath Castle Hostel € *Jenkinstown, County Kilkenny; tel: (056) 67674; <www.irelandyha.org>*. Ireland's oldest youth hostel in a 15th-century Norman Tower House with many medieval features and a magnificent dining room.

Hotel Kilkenny €–€€ *College Road, Kilkenny; tel: (056) 776 2000; fax: (056) 776 5984; <www.griffingroup.ie>*. Newly refurbished and set in planned gardens just outside the city, the Hotel Kilkenny has a light, contemporary design furnished with specially-commissioned Irish products.

LIMERICK AND SHANNON

Carrygerry Country House €€ *near Shannon Airport, Newmarket-on-Fergus, County Clare; tel: (061) 363739; fax: (061) 363823*. Converted 18th-century house with rooms set around a courtyard, and a fine conservatory restaurant. Irish breakfast included.

Castletroy Park Hotel €–€€ *Dublin Road, Limerick; tel: (061) 335566; fax: (061) 331117; <www.castletroy-park.ie>*. One of Limerick's most sought after hotels for conference facilities, but still capable of rolling out a proper welcome to leisure guests. The Merry Pedlar pub offers a chance for everyone to relax.

Dromoland Castle €€€ *Newmarket-on-Fergus, County Clare; tel: (061) 368144; fax: (061) 363355; <www.dromoland.ie>.* This luxury estate can trace its heritage back to Gaelic royalty via the O'Brians, once barons of Inchiquin, who were direct descendants of Brian Boru. Despite all this history, the hotel is welcoming, relaxing and mystical – especially the grounds of the castle which include a lake and delightful parklands.

Railway Hotel € *Parnell Street, Limerick; tel: (061) 413653; fax: (061) 419762; <www.railwayhotel.ie>.* Just opposite the rail and bus stations, this family-run hotel offers all the necessities and is well located to explore Limerick.

MAYO

Ashford Castle €€€ *Cong; tel: (094) 954 6003; fax: (094) 954 6260; <www.ashford.ie>.* The last word in luxury holiday accommodation, this former 19th-century mansion of the Guinness family is arguably Ireland's grandest castle hotel, with parts of it dating back to the early 13th century. The best rooms are at the top of the castle and offer views of Lough Corrib, the River Cong and the surrounding parkland.

Olde Railway Hotel € *The Mall, Westport; tel: (098) 25166; fax: (098) 25090; <www.anu.ie/railwayhotel>.* This very agreeable riverside hotel makes you feel instantly welcome and hardly lets you in the door before offering you a cup of tea. William Thackeray described it as 'one of the prettiest, comfortablest hotels in Ireland'. It's full of eccentric artefacts and bonhomie.

Quiet Man Hostel € *Abbey Street, Cong, County Mayo; tel: (092) 46089; fax: (092) 46448; <www.quietman-cong.com>.* Budget accommodation near to pubs, shops, the river and Cong Abbey.

WATERFORD

Granville Hotel €–€€ *Meagher Quay, Waterford; tel: (051) 305555; fax: (051) 305566; <www.granville-hotel.ie>.* Situated along Waterford's quayside and with as many historical connections as rooms, it's very popular with business travellers but makes a great base for exploring the town.

Lismore Hotel € *Main Street, Lismore; tel: (058) 54555; fax: (058) 53068; email: lismorehotel@eircom.net.* A pleasant hotel in a great setting along the Munster Blackwater river and in the historic centre of Lismore.

O'Grady's Restaurant & Guesthouse € *Cork Road, Waterford; tel: (051) 378851; fax: (051) 374062; <www.ogradys.ie>.* Bedrooms are all en suite. Michelin-recommended restaurant specialises in local seafood.

Tower Hotel € *The Mall, Waterford; tel: (051) 875801; fax: (051) 870129; <www.towerhotelwaterford.com>.* Luxury hotel in the city centre with amenities ranging from an indoor swimming pool to conference facilities.

Waterford Castle €€€ *The Island, Ballinakill, Waterford; tel: (051) 878203; fax: (051) 879316; <www.waterfordcastle.com>.* Historic castle situated on its own private island on the River Suir, surrounded by woodlands and an 18-hole championship golf course. 19 bright and airy bedrooms with stunning views of the estate.

WEXFORD

Marlfield House Hotel €€ *Gorey; tel: (055) 21124; fax: (055) 21572; <www.marfieldhouse.com>.* Stylish country mansion converted into an exquisite hotel that consistently wins awards for international hospitality. The accommodation is sumptuous and the restaurant a gourmand's dream. And the house itself is a stately home with no luxury spared.

Rosslare Great Southern Hotel €–€€ *Rosslare Harbour, County Wexford; tel: (053) 33233; fax: (053) 33543; <www.gshotels.com>.* Especially popular with families who come to enjoy the view over the clifftop and seaport.

NORTHWEST

Green Gate € *Ardvalley, Adara, Co Donegal; tel: (075) 41546.* This traditional cottage was bought by the proprietor as a writer's retreat. He's now made it a home away from home for himself and all those lucky enough to spend this night atop a hill on the edge of the Atlantic.

NORTHERN IRELAND

Belfast International Youth Hostel € *22–32 Donegall Road, Belfast BT12 5JN; tel: (028) 9031 5435; fax: (028) 9043 9699; <www.hini.org.uk>.* High-standard hostel in a central location.

Bushmills Inn € *9 Dunluce Road, Bushmills, County Antrim BT 57 8QG; tel: (028) 2073 2339; fax: (028) 2073 2048; <www. bushmillsinn.com>.* With all the ingredients of a good Irish holiday – whiskey, beds and great breakfasts – you could just stay here. However, with the Giant's Causeway only 3km (2 miles) away you should really get out to see it. Though recently refurbished, it still feels like a 19th-century coach house (minus the horses).

Culloden €€€ *142 Bangor Road, Holywood, County Down; tel: (028) 9042 1066; fax: (028) 9042 6777; <www.hastingshotels.com>.* Northern Ireland's most luxurious hotel is based on the shores of the Belfast Lough and boasts secluded gardens and woodland. In a most original touch, a glass cabinet shows off famous names that have stayed here – they've all signed plastic yellow ducks.

Europa €€–€€€ *Great Victoria Street, Belfast BT2 7AP; tel: (028) 9027 1066; fax: (028) 9032 7800; <www.hastingshotels. com>.* Next to the Grand Opera House, a 5-minute walk to the Golden Mile. Spacious elegance and stylish comfort.

Rathlin Guesthouse € *The Quay, Rathlin Island, Co. Antrim, BT54 6RT; tel: (028) 2076 3917.* In the most isolated spot in Northern Ireland, this bed and breakfast offers the only accommodation on Rathlin Island.

Recommended Restaurants

The choice of restaurants in Ireland has increased enormously over the last few years, with establishments offering Chinese, Indian, Japanese, Malaysian and Thai cuisine opening up in many areas. A few restaurants serve authentic Irish food, like cabbage and bacon or Dublin coddle (bacon, kidney, sausage and onion), and hotels and guesthouses often serve excellent, home-made food.

While Cork, including Kinsale, is acknowledged as one of the best areas for eating out, Belfast has developed hugely, and prices compete with those in the Republic. Some restaurants have a full licence to serve any drinks; otherwise, they serve wine only and not beer. Special tourist menus are a cheaper alternative for lunch and dinner.

The VAT rate on restaurant meals is 12½ (17½ in Northern Ireland) percent. In addition, some restaurants may add a 12½ percent service charge. To give you an idea of prices, we have used the following symbols for a three-course meal for one excluding wine:

€€€   over €40/£30

€€   €15–40/£10–30

€   under €15/£10

DUBLIN

Chapter One Restaurant €€–€€€ *18/19 Parnell Square, Dublin 1; tel: 873 2266; fax: 873 2330; <www.chapteronerestaurant.com>, open for lunches (12–2.30pm, Fri) and dinners (6–11pm, Tues–Sat).* This establishment, in the basement of the Dublin Writers Museum, is one of the city's best. The menu is classically French, but with a leaning toward Irish. It takes its cheeses and wines very seriously, and it shows. Located just across from the Gate Theatre, there are pre-theatre menus available from 6pm. Reservations advised.

Cornucopia € *19 Wicklow Street, Dublin 2; tel: 677 7583, open 8.30am–8pm Mon–Sat; Thur until 9pm; 12–6pm Sun.* A small self-service vegetarian restaurant offering delicious meals like Turkish bean casserole, tasty salads and wholemeal breads.

Elephant and Castle €–€€ *18 Temple Bar, Dublin 2; tel: 679 3121; fax: 679 1399, open 8am–11.30pm Mon–Fri; Sat from 10.30am; Sun from 12pm.* This is the most popular informal restaurant in the city. Quality burgers, salads and meals with more than a hint of Mexican or Thai influence. Vegetarian options.

Ernie's Restaurant €€€ *Mulberry Gardens, Donnybrook, Dublin 4; tel: 269 3300; fax: 269 3269, open Mon–Sat 12.30– 2pm; 7.30–10pm.* Interesting restaurant built around a mulberry tree, with the main dining room lined with contemporary Irish paintings – mostly of the Kerry countryside. The cooking and presentation is classical, with charcoal grill, and seafood and game in season; but contemporary Irish dishes seem to be finding their way onto the menu.

Old Dublin Restaurant €€–€€€ *90/91 Francis Street, Dublin 8; tel: 454 72028; fax: 454 1406, open lunch Mon–Fri, dinner Mon–Sat.* Specialising in Russian and Scandinavian recipes such as *novgorod* (beef chateaubriand with fried barley and caviar) and *pelmini* (small beef or veal dumplings in consommé), this is an unusual but long-established restaurant. Book in advance.

Pasta Fresca €€ *2–4 Chatham Street, Dublin 2; tel: 679 2402; fax: 668 4563, open Mon–Sat 11.30am–12am; Sun 12–10pm.* A popular and relaxed restaurant, serving, as the name suggests, virtually every possible combination of pasta and sauce plus thin-crust Italian pizzas.

CORK

Ballymaloe House €€€ *Shanagarry; tel: (021) 465 2531; fax: (021) 465 2021; <www.ballymaloe.ie> open 12–1.15pm, 7pm– 9.15pm.* Located on a farm and run by the Allen family, noted for their gourmet writing. Meals are served in the house's cosy dining rooms and waiting guests enjoy aperitifs in the conservatory.

It feels like home and you're even offered a second helping of the main course if you feel the urge. The cuisine fits the setting. It has few pretentions and perfects the tradition of Irish country food.

Mary Ann's Bar and Restaurant €€ *Castletownshend, County Cork; tel: (028) 36146; fax: (028) 36377, open daily 6–9pm and 12–2.30 for Sunday lunch in winter.* Seafood restaurant with cheaper menus served from the bar; the restaurant is set in a small, idyllic seaside village in West Cork.

Presidents' Restaurant €€ *Longueville House, near Mallow, Co. Cork; tel: (022) 47156; <www.longuevillehous. ie>, open 12pm–5pm, 6.30pm–9pm.* An upmarket 18th-century mansion is the setting for this restaurant, where portraits of Ireland's presidents line the walls. Its vineyard produces a wine similar to a Riesling.

GALWAY

Currach Restaurant €€ *Corrib Great Southern Hotel, Dublin Road, Renmore Galway; tel: (091) 755281; <www.gsh. ie>, open 7.30–10am, 1–2.15pm, 6.45–9pm.* A restaurant with fine views overlooking Galway Bay.

Galleon Restaurant €–€€ *Beside the Church, Salthill, Galway; tel: (091) 522963; fax: (091) 581240, open daily noon–11pm.* Well-priced menu of fish, steaks and Irish stew; served in a seaside setting.

Oyster Room €€ *Galway Great Southern Hotel, Eyre Square, Galway; tel: (091) 564041; <www.gsh.ie>, open 7.30–10am, 6.30–9:30pm (9pm on Sunday).* Noted restaurant in centre of the city, serving first-class cuisine.

KERRY

Chart House €€ *The Mall, Dingle; tel: (066) 915 2255; <www. charterhousedingle.com> open Wed–Mon 6.30–10pm.* Recent winner of Jameson's Host of the Year award, this informal restaurant makes you feel welcomed, in the way only the Irish can.

Doyles Seafood Restaurant & Townhouse €€ *John Street, Dingle; tel: (066) 915 1144; fax: (066) 915 1618; <www.doylesof dingle.com>, open Mon–Sat 6–10pm.* One of the country's best-known restaurants. Daily specials depend on the day's catch. It's cramped, but it's also full of life and character – a fun place to eat.

La Cascade, Sheen Falls Lodge Hotel €€€ *Kenmare; tel: (064) 41600; fax: (064) 41386 <www.sheenfallslodge.ie>, open daily 7–9.30pm.* The view of the waterfalls makes as much of an impact as the cuisine, especially when the falls are lit at night. The cuisine is modern Irish followed by classic puddings. The wine cellar is another point of pride with nearly 1,000 wines available. They also use its atmospheric setting to serve port in the evenings.

LIMERICK AND SHANNON

Doolin Café € *Doolin, Co. Clare; tel: (065) 707 4795.* A friendly, informal atmosphere is the hallmark of the Doolin Café in its seaside village location. It offers wholesome food and good music as well as a range of books to browse through.

Earl of Thomond Restaurant Dromoland Castle €€€ *Newmarket-on-Fergus, County Clare; tel: (061) 368144; fax: (061) 363355; <www.dromoland.ie>, open daily 7.30–9.30pm; plus 12.30–1.30pm Sun.* The dining room in Dromoland Castle is spectacular, with superb, elaborate table settings and grand chandeliers overhead; excellent backdrop for the gourmet cuisine.

Lindbergh Restaurant €€ *Shannon Catering, Shannon Airport, Co. Clare; tel: (061) 471444; fax: (061) 472602.* This spacious restaurant has very friendly staff who serve up a decent selection of traditional Irish dishes. A good place to try the ham for which Limerick is famous.

MacCloskey's €€ *Bunratty House Mews, Bunratty, Co. Clare. tel: (061) 364082; fax: (061) 364350, open Tue–Sat 7pm–4.30pm.* An exquisite gourmet cellar restaurant serving classic cuisine. Always bustling, it creates the ambience for a memorable evening.

Manuel's Restaurant €€ *Kilkee, Co. Clare; tel: (065) 56211, open daily from Easter to mid-Sept, 6.30–10.30pm.* Manuel's is a modern restaurant, with nautical decor. It specialises in seafood but also does lovely vegetarian dishes.

WATERFORD

Buggys Glencairn Inn € *Glencairn Lismore; tel: (058) 56232; <www.lismore.com>, open daily 7.15–9pm.* This fire-lit pub offers old-world bedrooms and hearty meals. Come early to ensure a table.

Dwyer's €€ *8 Mary Street, Waterford; tel: (051) 877478; fax: (051) 877480; <www.dwyersrestaurant.com>, open Mon–Sat 6–8pm.* Small but very chic gourmet restaurant with an original menu that changes every two weeks. The vegetables, meat, eggs and game are all sourced locally, while the the fish is bought at nightly auctions in nearby Dunmore East.

Ship €€ *Dock Road, Dunmore East; tel: (051) 383141; fax: (051) 383144, open daily 12.30–2pm; 7–10pm during summer; winter hours vary.* Fresh seafood served in the informal surroundings of an old Victorian house.

The Tannery Restaurant €€ *10 Quay Street, Dungarvan; tel: (058) 45420; fax: (058) 45118; <www.tannery.ie>, open Tues–Sun 12.30–2.30pm 6.30–9.30pm.* This converted leather warehouse has become one of the country's most stylish restaurants.

WEXFORD

Dunbrody Country House Hotel €€€ *Arthurstown; tel: (051) 389600; fax: (051) 389601; <www.dunbrodyhouse.com>, open daily Mon–Sat 6.30–9.15pm.* A blend of classical Irish cooking and continental charm served in a setting that overlooks an organic vegetable and fruit garden.

La Marine at Kelly's Resort Hotel €€ *Rosslare; tel: (053) 32114; fax: (053) 32222, open daily 12.30–3pm, 6.30–9.30pm.*

Reservations are essential at this contemporary restaurant, as it's considered the place in which to be seen by the locals. The contemporary-style food is delicious, and the wine list is enticing.

Marlfield House Hotel €€ *Courtown Road, Gorey; tel: (055) 21124; fax: (055) 21572; <www.marlfieldhouse.com>, open daily 7–9pm; Sun 12.30–1.45.* The menu at this gorgeous and well-renowned country house is mainly classic French or Mediterranean with a twist. Fish, including wild salmon, Bannow Bay oysters and Wexford mussels, is a strong point. Fresh herbs, vegetables and fruit are picked from Marlfield's own gardens, which are popular with visitors. A delightful dining experience.

WICKLOW

Hunter's Hotel €€–€€€ *Newrath Bridge, Rathnew; tel: (0404) 40106; fax: (0404) 40338; e-mail <reception@ hunters.ie>, open daily 1–2.30pm, 7.30–9pm.* Hunter's Hotel is an historic 18th-century coaching inn with fine gardens. The food here is simple but impressive traditional Irish fare.

Kitty's of Arklow €€ *56 Main Street, Arklow; tel: (0402) 31669; fax: (0402) 31553, open daily 6–10pm.* This retro-style bar stands in Arklow's city centre and is something of an institution.

Old Rectory Country House & Restaurant €€ *Wicklow Town, County Wicklow; tel: (0404) 67048 fax: (0404) 69181, closed Jan–Feb.* Fine, imaginative cooking, often made or garnished with edible herbs or flowers, is on offer at this attractive Victorian country house.

Pizza del Forno € *The Mall Centre, Main Street, Wicklow Town; Tel: (0404) 67075, closed Christmas–mid-Feb.* An excellent family restaurant that is attractively decorated with red gingham tablecloths. Serves tasty pizzas, steaks and vegetarian dishes.

The Roundwood Inn €€ *Roundwood; tel: (01) 281 8107, open Fri–Sat 7.30–9.30pm, Sun 1–2pm.* The Roundwood serves dishes

influenced by German cuisine. Also does good bar food, with
options including goulash, Irish stew and smoked salmon.

NORTHERN IRELAND

Cayenne Restaurant €€ *7 Ascot House, Shaftesbury Square,
Belfast BT2 7DB; tel: (028) 9033 1532; fax: (028) 9026 1575;
<www.cayennerestaurant.com>, open Mon–Fri 12–2.30pm, 6–
11pm; dinner only Sat.* The reasonably priced fine food served at
the Cayenne Restaurant has proved a popular equation with
Belfast's diners. There's a good wine list and a bar so stylish that
you may forget you're waiting for a table.

Hastings Slieve Donard Hotel €€ *Downs Road, Newcastle,
County Down BT33 0AH; tel: (028) 4372 1066; fax: (028) 4372
4830; <www.hastingshotels.com>.* The Peray French Inn at the
entrance to the hotel is a welcoming and popular venue, serving
pub lunch and dinner fare.

La Belle Epoque €€ *61 Dublin Road, Belfast BT2 7HE; tel:
(028) 9032 3244, open Mon–Fri 12–11pm; Sat from 5pm.* Classic
French gourmet restaurant that serves game in season.

Portaferry Hotel €€ *The Strand, Portaferry, Co. Down BT22
1PE; tel: (028) 4272 8231; fax: (028) 4272 8999, open daily
12.30–2.30pm, 5.30–9pm; Sat until 10pm.* The Portaferry Hotel is
in a pleasant quayside spot and does fresh seafood, including
stuffed mussels, fried oysters and turbot. The pub serves a good
selection of bar food.

Restaurant Michael Deane €€€ *34–40 Howard Street, Belfast
BT1 6PR. tel: (028) 9038 1655, <www.deanesbelfast.com>, open
Mon–Sat 12–2.30pm, 6–10pm.* Deane's restaurant offers perhaps
the best fine-dining experience in Belfast and was the first place in
Ireland to be awarded a Michelin star. There are two dining options
here: the discreet, elegant, Michelin-starred restaurant upstairs and
the lively, chic brasserie on the ground floor. Both offer meticulously prepared modern cuisine covering all continents.

INDEX